Contagious Faith

Philip F. Lawler

Contagious Faith

Why the Church Must Spread Hope,
Not Fear, in a Pandemic

CRISIS
PUBLICATIONS

Manchester, New Hampshire

Crisis Publications

Box 5284, Manchester, NH 03108

1-800-888-9344

www.CrisisMagazine.com

paperback ISBN 978-1-64413-511-2

ebook ISBN 978-1-64413-512-9

Library of Congress Control Number: 2021933592

First printing

To our grandchildren,
whose hopes for tomorrow
rest on our decisions today

Contents

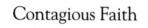

Contagious Faith

Introduction

Living Dangerously

Fear is contagious.

Sometime early in 2020 — at different times for different people — we Americans learned about Covid: a disease unlike anything we had experienced. We heard expert predictions that the disease would cause millions of fatalities. We saw the projections. We calculated the odds that the victims would include our friends, our relatives, ourselves. And we were afraid.

Although a disease of this sort was new to us, dwarfing any public health crisis in recent memory, it was not without historic precedent. Even by the most pessimistic estimates, the Covid epidemic never figured to be as deadly as the Spanish flu of 1918. But our fears, amplified by the mass media, were much more pronounced than the justifiable fears of our ancestors a century ago. Our responses were more extreme. The disease itself was not as damaging as the flu of 1918, but the effect on society was far more debilitating.

Why?

The thesis of this book is that in the Covid crisis of 2020, the fear of the disease was deadlier than the disease itself. And the fear, in turn, was caused by a lack of faith. As a society, we had drained down the reservoir of Christian belief that would have given us hope to balance our fears. When the crisis arose, sad to say, even Christians succumbed to the epidemic of fear.

The Covid crisis challenged Christians to examine our consciences. Did we surrender to a fear that is foreign to, and unworthy of, our status as children of a loving God? Did we fail to offer an attractive alternative to fear, a balance to the climate of despair, a witness to hope? Did we show, by our actions, a living faith that could inspire others: a faith that could balance the fear of disease, a faith that might be contagious?

Whom Should I Fear?

What are your greatest fears? What secret terrors keep you awake at night? Do you worry about the prospect of natural disaster, violent crime, disease, lost love, financial collapse, or social ostracism? These are all legitimate reasons for worry. But in most cases, you can recover from these setbacks. Death is different; fear of death is a different sort of fear because from death there can be no recovery.

But wait: Jesus tells us that He has overcome death. He even gives us the formula: "the bread which comes down from heaven, that a man may eat of it and not die." He assures us that "he who eats my flesh and drinks my blood has eternal life" (John 6: 50, 54). So death does *not* draw down the final curtain; death is *not* the greatest tragedy, the thing that we should fear the most.

There *is* something worse than death: damnation. And from that, there *is* no recovery. But Christian faith brings the good news that damnation—the final failure, the greatest legitimate fear—can be avoided. Our faith, our Church, brings us the means of salvation and, therefore, the reservoir of hope.

Unfortunately, we live in a post-Christian society marked by a lack of the lively faith that inspires hope. Formed by secularism, our neighbors search for some form of salvation on this earth, where none will be found.

The Pagan Approach

In an intriguing new book entitled *American Awakening: Identity Politics and Other Afflictions of Our Time*, Joshua Mitchell, a Georgetown University political scientist, compares the political conflicts of America today with the ritual of ancient pagan societies. Those ancient peoples, he remarks, sought scapegoats to take the blame for the evils in the world and made war to suppress or eradicate (dare I say to "cancel"?) the people identified as scapegoats. Christians countered that primitive approach by teaching that the source of evils is in ourselves, in our own failings, in Original Sin. Christians, when they are behaving as Christians, do not blame others for their woes.

But in 2021, the Western world is not really Christian—not in its fundamental beliefs, not in its behavior. So when we faced Covid, an enemy we did not know how to fight, we relapsed into the behavior that Mitchell saw as characteristic of paganism: looking for scapegoats, blaming the people who failed to wear masks or maintain the approved social distancing. We looked to government for a solution because we have become accustomed to asking government for solutions to our problems. But the government cannot eliminate disease. So we took another step toward the pagans and looked for someone to blame.

Ordinarily, if someone dies in a natural disaster or loses a battle with a natural disease, no one is to blame. But in the supercharged political atmosphere of 2020, there were charges and countercharges galore: unfounded claims that politicians bore the blame for Covid deaths. Worse, there arose a general suspicion of one's neighbors, a fear that any stranger might be the source of the disease that could kill. Once again, the fear was more dangerous than the disease, and (as I shall argue) the political response was more deleterious to public health than the virus.

The Good Samaritan

Christians should never have fallen in with a secular society's panicked reaction to Covid, never accepted the counsels of fear. We should always have maintained a healthy skepticism toward the notion that our government can solve our problems. We should be mindful that there will always be problems—including some grave problems, and certainly including natural death—in this world. But we have overcome the world.

Instructed by the parable of the Good Samaritan, we Christians have been trained to see all men as our neighbors, especially those in need. We should recoil from the notion that "social distancing"—isolating ourselves from others, especially potential carriers of the virus—is an elegant solution. We should be bringing health and hope to others, seeking out rather than avoiding personal contact. And the best help we can offer is our faith, our hope. "Say to those who are of fearful heart, Be strong, fear not!" (Isa. 35:4).

To help our neighbors, however, we must first strengthen ourselves. We cannot spread our faith if we do not live our faith. We need the help of grace. We need the sacraments. And in the greatest tragedy of the Covid era, access to the life-giving sacraments of Christ's Church was choked off during this time when we needed it most.

To bring the gift of hope to our neighbors, we must be able to show that our Faith is alive and real: that we practice what we preach. We must demonstrate to them that our life in Faith—our life in the sacraments—is our top priority, that our spiritual health is more important to us than our physical health. Sadly, that is not the story of the Catholic Church in the Covid era.

Infectious diseases are an unhappy reality of life on this earth. They arise unpredictably, spark fears, take their toll, and eventually subside. In 2020 the world was paralyzed by the Covid epidemic. But worse diseases, more infectious and much deadlier, have swept the world in the past. Many people died, but our societies and their institutions survived. We mourned and moved on. Not so in 2020; something utterly unprecedented happened in response to Covid.

By the time you read this book, I hope and pray that the Covid epidemic will have subsided. But inevitably there will be another epidemic in our future. How will we respond? I write now in the hope that we — especially we Christians, we Catholics — will learn to respond more appropriately, to help our neighbors escape—not just from the disease that afflicts the body but from the more dangerous disease that afflicts the soul.

A *Thought Experiment*

Just to help clarify our thinking, let's imagine an unpleasant possibility: that we learned, late in 2020, that sooner or later we would all be infected with the Covid virus.

This isn't an outlandish idea. Masks and social distancing hadn't stopped the spread of the disease. The virus had continued to spread — at an accelerated rate, toward the end of the year — despite painful and intrusive government restrictions on our behavior. The vaccines that were just becoming available were unproven at best; they may not work, and their potential side effects were daunting. Experts (some experts, anyway) were telling us that herd immunity was not a realistic prospect for the foreseeable future.

There are other experts who said that we were actually very close to herd immunity. Although their arguments were largely ignored by the mainstream media (which prefer the sensational bad news) and by ambitious politicians (who enjoy their new-found control), I found these experts more persuasive. But here I am not addressing the scientific arguments—which I am not competent to assess in any case. I am conducting a thought experiment. *What if* we were all going to be infected?

So put yourself back in, say, December 2020. Suppose that you *know* that eventually you will have the disease. If you are in reasonably good health, it's very unlikely that Covid will kill you. You might have no symptoms at all. Or you might be miserable for a few days, even a few weeks. There may be some lingering effects. But you'll probably live.

If you *know* your day with the disease is coming, you can do a few things to increase the likelihood of a quick recovery. Eat a healthy diet. Make sure you're getting plenty of vitamin D. Exercise regularly. Don't smoke. Use alcohol in moderation. In other words, you can do your best to stay healthy, with your immune system functioning at its best. But of course, you should do all that anyway.

Should you wear a mask, keep your distance, stay at home? Not for your own sake. What would be the point? In our scenario, you know that you will contract the virus someday. Why postpone the inevitable? You may even prefer to catch a mild dose right away, while you're feeling fit. Who knows? A more virulent strain of the disease might be coming, and people who have already survived one bout will probably be immune. Although you're healthy now, who knows what medical problems might crop up in the future, so that you won't be ready to combat the infection? All things considered, it may seem better to live your normal life, accepting the fact that some day you will be infected.

Do It for Others

You've been encouraged to wear a mask for the sake of others, though, on the theory that you might be infected without know-ing it, and thus you could pass along the virus to others. In our scenario this logic is questionable, too. If everyone is doomed to catch Covid sooner or later, how much should you sacrifice to postpone someone else's day of reckoning? For the vast majority, a bout with Covid will be an inconvenience. Does that sound insensitive? Bear in mind that most of the people who contract the virus will experience no noteworthy symptoms. Granted, others will suffer though something more than just an ordinary "inconvenience." But you can't prevent that.

Ah, but there is another scenario, and it's one that has been sketched for you again and again. Even though you feel fine, you *could* be infected unawares, and you *might* pass along the virus to someone else, and that someone *could* be vulnerable, and so you *might* be indirectly and unintentionally responsible for a Covid fatality. The odds are heavily stacked against that prospect, but it is not impossible. Needless to say, you don't want to be responsible for a neighbor's untimely death.

Now wait; let's take a careful look at the ground we've just covered. What is an "untimely" death, in this context or any other? (Is there ever such a thing as a "timely" death?) We shall all face death; we just don't know when. "Watch, therefore, for you know neither the day nor the hour," Jesus warns us (Matt. 25:13).

Catholics boldly proclaim that every human being has the right to life. But no one has a "right" to escape death. We cannot protect our neighbors from the prospect of death by natural causes, and disease is a natural cause. *Of course* we avoid actions that would be likely to spread disease, and so responsible people stay home when they are sick. But we cannot eliminate every possible avenue of infection. As long as people live with others, some disease will spread and for some, the disease will be fatal.

Approaching Death

Let me take my thought-experiment one step further. Imagine that — contrary to fact — you could predict the time of your own death. Imagine that you *knew* that you would be dead in a month. Would you want to isolate yourself from your neighbors, friends, and relatives? Would you withdraw from social life entirely? Instead, wouldn't you want to do what you could, while you could, to enjoy the company of those you love?

Or suppose you knew that you would be dead within a year, but the exact date could be sooner or later, depending on what precautions you took. *Then* would you withdraw, to stay alone in a sterile room and try to stretch out your term on earth as long as possible? Or would you still want to live a normal life? How many weeks of normalcy would you trade for an extra week of isolation?

Stonewall Jackson was renowned not only for his strategic brilliance but also for his personal bravery in battle. When asked how he could appear untroubled by the shells that burst around him, he answered: "God has fixed the time for my death. I do not concern myself about that, but to be always ready, no matter when it may overtake me." That's good advice for anyone to follow.

St. Charles Borromeo was playing a friendly game of chess when someone asked him: "If you were told that you were about to die, what would you do?" He answered: "I would finish this game of chess. I began it for the glory of God, and I would end it with the same intention." He had his spiritual affairs in order; he saw no reason to panic.

Our society needs the courage of Jackson, the confidence of St. Charles. In an era living under the shadow of despair, our people need hope. Not hope in a vaccine or hope in a political policy, but hope that is enduring, hope that is not shaken by earthly worries. That hope will only be found in Jesus Christ. We Christians, charged with the mission of bringing that hope to the world, must provide that hope.

The Beacon of Hope

If fear is contagious, so is faith. But to be contagious—to attract others, to light up the beacon of hope—faith must be lived with courage and confidence. Jesus taught his disciples to live their faith boldly:

> You are the salt of the earth; but if salt has lost its taste, how shall its saltness be restored? It is no longer good for anything except to be thrown out and trodden under foot by men. You are the light of the world. A city set on a hill cannot be hid. Nor do men light a lamp and put it under a bushel, but on a stand, and it gives light to all in the house. (Matt. 5:13-16)

"Do not be afraid," said Pope John Paul II, as he began the homily at the Mass inaugurating his pontificate. That same phrase, that same directive—"Do not be afraid"—occurs twenty-nine times in the Bible. Again and again, God tells his people not to shrink from confrontations with worldly powers and worldly problems. The Lord assures His faithful that He will support them with His own almighty power.

"Do not be afraid," Jesus tells his first disciples, as they reel in astonishment after a display of his power over nature; "henceforth you will be catching men" (Luke 5:10). With assurance of the Lord's help, Christians should not shrink from the troubles of our day. We should recognize them as opportunities to bring our neighbors closer to God.

The year 2020 was not a happy one for Americans. The Covid menace was not the only trauma that we suffered. Our political system was strained to the breaking point; our cities were battle zones; our confidence in our future as a nation was shattered. Too many people lived in fear—not only fear of Covid but a more general fear for the future.

In the past Christianity has often grown—sometimes at a spectacular rate—during times of societal crisis. The dispirited people of Jerusalem, living unhappily under Roman domination, were ready to hear the message of St. Peter on the first Pentecost. A few centuries later, as the Roman empire collapsed, the city's people noticed that the small band of Christians, enduring through persecution, offered far more hope than the old gods or the new Goths. Today the modern world cries out for a new introduction to the hope that our faith can bring.

To make that introduction, however, we Christians must cast off our own unhealthy fears. Our neighbors must see us living with the confidence proper to children of God. If we Catholics profess that the Eucharist is the "source and summit" of our spiritual lives, our neighbors must see us making sacrifices and even running risks to attend Mass and receive the Eucharist. They must see our devotion—not as a cold pious display but as a source of energy that sustains our lives. Faith is contagious when those who lack faith become curious about those who do and, finally, realize that in an era clouded by despair, Jesus Christ offers the only real hope.

Will we find a cure for Covid? I don't know. But we already have a cure for the Covid panic — if only we will share it.

1

The Empty Square

Friday evening, March 27, 2020. The sun had already set in Rome at the end of a cold, blustery, raw, rainy day. St. Peter's Square was dark and all the more forbidding because it was empty—but for one man.

Pope Francis walked alone across the windswept square, a bit hunched over, with his mild but noticeable limp. There were no acolytes beside him, no other prelates to assist him at the altar. Invoking God's protection against the scourge of the coronavirus, he raised a monstrance containing the Blessed Sacrament, and with it gave his blessing *Urbi et Orbi*: to the city and the world.

"No director could have created such a powerful scene," said the Italian screenwriter Massimiliano Perrotta—who has made it his life's work to create powerful scenes. Here was a single man, a tiny figure in the vast square that can accommodate tens of thousands; an AP report described him as "utterly alone before an invisible enemy." The darkness, the silence, the inclement weather all contributed to the ominous sense that this lone man, standing for all mankind, was facing an enormous and implacable foe.

But then there was one even more powerful factor, cutting through the gloom, promising to dispel the darkness: the Lord of the universe, present in the Eucharist, the source of all hope.

No believing Catholic could doubt the effective power of the papal blessing. Pope Francis was wielding the infinite power of the Eucharist, the source and summit of our faith. The faithful could draw comfort and confidence in Christ's protection.

Still, powerful as it was, there was something missing from this scene. The pope was alone, but the Eucharist is meant to be shared. This was a religious ritual without a congregation. The pope was blessing the people: the people of Rome and the people of the world.

But the people weren't there.

Two days earlier, in a public audience on the feast of the Annunciation, the pontiff had asked all the world's faithful to join him in prayer on this day. But he had asked them to join him remotely, watching the ceremony on television or the internet. St. Peter's Square had been closed to the public.

All through Rome—and soon, all around the world—Catholic churches had closed their doors. In a stunning development, without any precedent in the history of the Church, the faithful were prevented from attending the Mass, barred from the sacraments, not by secular persecutors but by the choice of their own bishops. Two weeks later, during Holy Week, as they faced the bleak prospect of an Easter without a Mass, devout Catholics could feel the sorrow of Mary Magdalen, weeping at the empty tomb: "Because they have taken away my Lord, and I do not know where they have laid Him" (John 20:13).

An Interlude or a Trend

This is a book about a time when leaders of the Catholic Church told their people *not* to come to church. A time when Church leaders encouraged the public to think that the preservation of physical health should take precedence over the needs of spiritual growth. A time when some of the most zealous Catholics resisted their leaders' message. A time when the Catholics who are ordinarily most docile to Church authority found themselves deliberately circumventing their bishops' directives, in order to receive the sacraments.

Was that dramatic March 27 ceremony in St. Peter's Square a harbinger of what was to come in the Catholic Church: with the pope alone, with the people absent? Did this eerie interlude expose some serious differences between the hierarchy and the faithful, or between contrasting understandings of what the Church is and does? When pastors advise parishioners not to come to Sunday Mass, not to worry about confession, not to marry and baptize, can they reasonably expect the people to return to the sacraments once (if ever) the crisis ends? What does the Catholic Church have to offer to the faithful and to the world at large, in a time of crisis, in the face of worldwide fear? Has the Church been faithful to her mission and fulfilled her role in the time of need? Or has She missed an opportunity to spread the Gospel, to bring hope to a world on the brink of despair? These are the questions that I explore in the pages that follow.

My opinions are my own. I claim no special authority. I have only the mandate that applies to every baptized Christian, to do my best to spread the faith, to read the signs of the times as best I can. My conclusions may be wrong. In fact, I hope they are wrong because their implications are distressing. If I am mistaken, I hope that better analysts and better Christians (of whom there are many) will provide better answers to my questions. But the questions must be asked, and they should be answered.

Before I ask my questions and pose my answers, let me introduce myself, so that you, the reader, can understand something of my perspective.

Through the Eyes of Faith

To understand me, you must begin with my Catholic faith because it is the most important thing about me. And the most important thing about the Faith, the "source and summit" of Catholic spiritual life, is the Eucharist. The Mass is not just a group prayer service, not just a ceremony performed to make the participants feel better. It is the celestial banquet, the central reality of the universe, in which Jesus Christ becomes present to the faithful, to give glory to the Father.

At a dinner party some years ago, when an acquaintance commented that the Eucharist is a beautiful symbol, the writer Flannery O'Connor famously burst out: "Well, if it's a symbol, to hell with it." She later wrote to a friend, explaining:

> That was all the defense I was capable of but I realize now
> that this is all I will ever be able to say about it, outside
> of a story, except that it is the center of existence for me;
> all the rest is expendable.

That is the Catholic faith as I understand it, as I try to live it. For nearly forty years, I have tried to attend Mass every day. Participating in the Mass is not an obligation for me; it is an astonishing privilege, a blessing beyond all understanding. For me, too, the Mass is the central focus of my day, the central focus of my life, without which I am lost.

For roughly the same forty years I have worked full-time as a journalist covering Catholic affairs. I have seen the best and the worst of the Catholic Church: the luminous signs of God's grace and the depressing evidence of man's sin.

As a journalist I have often needed that focus, to maintain a lively faith in the midst of scandal. I began writing about the sexual abuse of children by Catholic priests in the early 1990s, nearly a full decade before the *Boston Globe* splashed that ugly topic across the headlines of the mainstream media. For years I explored the trails of clerical abuse, searching for an explanation of how such depravity had been tolerated, even protected, by Church leaders.

In *The Faithful Departed*, published in 2008, I offered the best explanation I could muster. Church leaders, I wrote, had lost confidence in the transcendent power of the faith. During an era of dramatic cultural change, they had shrunk from confrontation, allowing secular thought to guide the Church. In a vain bid for public approval, they had avoided hard truths. They thought that by compromising the integrity of the faith they might gain social standing. It didn't work, and it could never work, because the integrity of the Faith—the enduring witness for truth—is the only reason why society would respect the Church.

So when they learned of priests molesting children, bishops treated the abuse as a public relations problem to be managed rather than an evil to be eradicated. They thought, by covering up the evidence, they could avoid a scandal—and thus they brought upon themselves and upon Christ's Church a far more damaging scandal.

Shaken by Scandals

The sex-abuse scandal horrified me, as it horrified so many others. I was appalled to learn that many priests had been engaged in such abominable behavior, then still more appalled to realize that many bishops had failed to protect their people. In fact, many bishops had *lied* to their people: betraying the confidence of the faithful, betraying the truth, betraying the witness of Christ who assured us that the truth would make us free.

The "Long Lent" of 2002, when the full extent of the sex-abuse scandal was exposed, prompted many thousands of disillusioned Catholics to leave the Church. Anyone familiar with my work knows that I was unsparing in my criticism of the bishops who allowed and abetted (and in some cases joined in) the sinful and criminal activities of clerics under their supervision, the betrayal of the innocent. (As a friend put it, "they don't make millstones big enough.") But I can honestly say that as saddened and sickened as I was by the corruption, it never shook my faith. I could still distinguish between the sacramental life of the Church, the Bride of Christ, and the perfidy of the weak men—sinners like myself—who serve and guide and sometimes traduce the faithful.

The year 2020 was different. This year, the "Long Lent" of the Covid lockdown shook my faith.

In the sex-abuse scandal, corrupt prelates were guided by their own self-interest (and a misguided self-interest at that) rather than by the good of the Church, the welfare of souls. Still the sacramental life of the Church continued. The faithful still had access to Mass, to confession, to baptism. Young couples were married, the sick and aged were anointed. The churches were open for private prayer and visits to the Blessed Sacrament. There were liturgical abuses, but the eucharistic liturgy was offered regularly in every parish. There was corruption, but the corruption did not cut off the ordinary flow of sacramental life.

Not so this year. The churches were closed. Weddings and funerals were postponed. The elderly died alone, without benefit of the sacraments. The faithful were barred from attending Mass. The sacramental life of the Church was suppressed—not by persecuting tyrants but by our own bishops.

Again and again, as the lockdown continued, and as the first tentative reopening of the churches met with resistance, I asked myself how this could happen. The most fundamental duty of bishops is to administer the sacraments. How could they let *anything* else take precedence over that sacred duty?

In a message to the Catholic bishops of the United States, in January 2012, Pope Benedict XVI delivered a solemn warning:

> It is imperative that the entire Catholic community in the United States come to realize the grave threats to the Church's public moral witness presented by a radical secularism which finds increasing expression in the political and cultural spheres. The seriousness of these threats needs to be clearly appreciated at every level of ecclesial life. Of particular concern are certain attempts being made to limit that most cherished of American freedoms, the freedom of religion.

Just eight years later, our freedom to practice our Catholic faith was compromised, in part by government mandates but also, and even more frighteningly, by Catholic bishops and pastors who were acting in response to secular pressures and worldly fears.

Yes, we faced a frightening epidemic. But for bishops of the Catholic Church, the spiritual health of their flock is even more important than physical health. Yes, prudence dictated some special measures, to protect against the spread of a potentially deadly virus. But our bishops were all too willing to accept unquestioningly the advice of secular public health experts, without weighing how that advice might conflict with the mission of the Church. Once again, Church leaders were following the guidance of the secular culture.

It is sad for the Church when Catholic prelates take their cues from the half-truths of a materialistic society. It is sad for that society, too, to lose the perspective that could be offered by a stalwart Catholic witness. Especially in a time of crisis, in a society that has become captive to fear, the world needs the perspective of the Church, reminding us that death need not be a terror, that Jesus Christ beckons us toward a happier eternal life. The world needs the encouragement that only the Church gives: "Be not afraid."

2

Who Closed the Churches?

A great silence spreads over the Christian world each year on Good Friday, to be broken by the explosive joy of the Gloria at the Easter vigil. But in 2020, when Holy Week arrived, the silence had been with us already for a few weeks, with churches closed and public liturgical celebrations banned.

Every year, Easter brings out the most magnificent and joyful liturgical celebration the Church can manage. The Alleluia that was suppressed during Lent is sung again — and often. The Gloria, too, is sung after having been omitted for forty days, now accompanied by the ringing of bells. But in 2020 there was to be no singing because there were no choirs, no congregations. The Easter Mass was celebrated by a lonely priest, facing a video camera in an empty church.

By early April, 24 American states had issued emergency regulations that restricted religious services; others soon followed. Diocesan officials meekly complied, and within a matter of weeks it was nearly impossible for a lay Catholic American to find a place where he could attend Mass without violating orders from the local government, the local diocese, or both.

The Mass was not banned, as it might have been under overt political persecution. Priests were authorized to celebrate Mass privately, and soon many were offering the faithful some solace by televising their "private" Mass or streaming the liturgy online. Pope Francis made his own daily Mass available to the world online. Bishops celebrated Mass in their cathedrals—which were otherwise empty except for his assistants and his videographers. Still, when Mass was celebrated, the lay faithful were not invited. On the contrary, they were told in no uncertain terms to stay away.

Past Precedents?

In defense of their extraordinary edicts, bishops observed that there was some precedent for closing churches during an epidemic. For example, they pointed out that when the plague hit Milan in 1576, the city's archbishop, the great St. Charles Borromeo, closed the cathedral.

Indeed he did. But St. Charles Borromeo, having determined that the confined space of the cathedral was unsafe, celebrated Mass in public squares. Believing that the epidemic was "a scourge sent by heaven," for which fervent prayer was the best response, he organized processions through the city's streets. He exhorted his priests to bring the sacraments to the sick, promising them that if they contracted the plague themselves, "it will be a quicker attainment of blessed glory." And he assured the frightened people of Milan: "If someone does contract the disease, and others are no longer there, then I myself—who will be going out among you every day, on account of the sick—will be there."

That was definitely *not* the message the American faithful were hearing in the spring of 2020. They were being told that the administration of the sacraments would be suspended until further notice. Canon lawyer Edward Peters remarked that this suspension of the sacraments was in effect a form of "territorial interdict," the canonical penalty "whereby Church authority could shut down access to the sacraments for the innocent as well as the guilty in whole countries." It was odd, to say the least, that prelates would revive the interdict, a canonical device that had not been invoked for generations, especially so because the penalty was imposed without any evidence of a canonical violation to warrant it. Still, Peters said, the novelty of the situation did not necessarily mean that bishops lacked the authority, under the Code of Canon Law, to suspend sacramental ministry for prudential reasons.

However, Peters continued, "I know of no authority whereby an arch/bishop can 'suspend' the operation of a sacrament itself, so I can only conclude that whenever a proper, willing minister utters the correct form while applying the necessary matter to an eligible, willing recipient, the sacrament occurs." In other words, if lay Catholics could find willing priests, they *could* receive the sacraments—with or without their bishop's permission. Before the lockdowns began, I had written that "I need to participate regularly in the holy Sacrifice; without it, life makes no sense. So if the Mass goes 'underground,' so will I." Many other faithful Catholics went underground in 2020.

The Underground Church

Some priests went "underground," too—or at least violated their bishops' directives—explaining that they felt morally obligated to perform their ministerial duties for the welfare of their people. In one extreme case, a Welsh priest, Father Sebastian Jones, witnessed the wedding of a couple belonging to the nomadic ethnic group known as the Travelers, explaining that he did so to "protect individuals and families from grave consequences that are particular to them" if they did not marry in the Church. (He was presumably referring to the risk that the couple, denied a wedding, might engage in sexual relations, thereby incurring both the burden of grave sin and the contempt of their very traditional community.) Archbishop George Stack of Cardiff said that he was "very shocked and upset" that the priest had "succumbed to that pressure." But Father Jones stood firm: "If the supreme law of the Church is the salvation of souls, then I have broken no law that I can suffer for eternally."

Actually, although they almost certainly did not know it, that Traveler couple probably did not require the presence of Father Jones to perform a sacramental marriage. The Code of Canon Law (#1116) provides that an eligible couple who intend "to enter a true marriage can validly and lawfully contract in the presence of witnesses" if they cannot arrange for a priest's presence within a month. A few priests, to my knowledge, advised engaged couples to do exactly that during the lockdown, when church weddings were forbidden, and to let the ecclesiastical paperwork catch up to their union later. Similarly, parents certainly had the right, and arguably the duty, to baptize their own children if—as happened for weeks in 2020—priests declined to perform the ceremony.

In Wales a few months later, after churches had been tentatively opened but threatened with another shutdown, another doughty priest, Father David Palmer, announced that he was ready to defy orders: "I will be arrested before I deny the sacraments to the people of God again," he announced on his Twitter account. "And I repent for having backed down before. Eternal life comes before this life... or our faith means nothing."

Ambiguity in Authority

A priest should never back down from his responsibility to administer the sacraments. But at the same time, a priest should be docile to orders from his bishop—remembering that on the day of his ordination, he swore obedience to the bishop and to his successors. So conscientious priests, faced with orders to close down their churches and stop celebrating Mass for the people, naturally questioned whether those orders were coming from their bishops or from secular authorities. All too often the answer was not clear.

In Rome, the situation *should* have been clear, since the Roman Pontiff exercises political as well as spiritual authority over the territory of the Vatican city-state. But in practice it was not easy to say whether the Vatican was acting independently or accepting orders from the city that surrounded it. On March 10, the police of Rome closed off access to St. Peter's Square at noon. Just a few hours later, the Vatican announced that St. Peter's basilica would be closed to visitors. Was that a decision freely made by Church officials? Vatican spokesmen said that it was. But the Vatican had been presented by the city with a fait accompli, since visitors could no longer reach the basilica. If the Vatican had lodged any objection to the Roman police action—which amounted to the unilateral closing of a recognized border—that protest was made very quietly.

Of course, Pope Francis and his designated subordinates have every right to close off access to Vatican territory if they deem that measure necessary. Bishops, too, have the authority to close churches and to regulate the sacramental life of the Church. But with the lines frequently blurred between orders from secular and ecclesiastical authorities, during this time of worldwide crisis, another question arose: When should the Catholic Church bow to orders from the state?

I offer a simple answer to that question: Never.

The Church can and should respect the authority of the state to protect public health—*provided* that the state's demands do not threaten the Church's central mission. Parish churches should be built in compliance with zoning regulations and fire codes; making the buildings safe does not compromise the administration of the sacraments or the work of evangelization.

But what happens when a public health emergency—like this current epidemic—prompts public officials to issue emergency regulations that *do* interfere with sacramental ministry? Then bishops and pastors must navigate a tricky course, respecting the rightful authority of the state without forfeiting the rightful (and greater) authority of the Church.

As mayors and governors tightened restrictions on public meetings, many bishops followed suit, with directives that limited—in some cases virtually eliminated—public access to the sacraments. So another conflict arose: a conflict between the undoubted authority of the bishop to set standards for ministry in his diocese and the equally certain right of the laity to have access to the sacraments.

"Sacred ministers cannot deny the sacraments to those who seek them at appropriate times, are properly disposed, and are not prohibited by law from receiving them," reads the Code of Canon Law (843). Now lay Catholics, in good standing with the Church—Catholics who were receiving the sacraments on a regular basis just a few days earlier, with no questions asked—were being turned away.

The Pastor's Quandry

Parish priests were caught in the middle of this conflict. Should they obey a directive from the bishop's office, if they thought that directive unjustly deprived the faithful of the sacraments?

In an analysis of the question for the Catholic News Agency site, J. D. Flynn and Ed Condon, both trained in canon law, summarized the difficulties and found: "And some priests have begun considering a question they never expected to find themselves asking: 'Should I obey my bishop?'"

Edward Peters, a leading canon law scholar whose blog provided invaluable insights on this crisis, suggested that it was time to take a deep breath. A priest is not obligated to respect an illegal order from his bishop, he acknowledged. However, Peters cautioned: "Do not assume that some wrong, even stupid, policies being announced by various levels of Church government are necessarily canonically *illegal* policies." He recommended that priests and laypeople alike should be "very wary" of the claim that any authoritative directive can be ignored.

But notice that Peters did not deny that in at least some cases a directive *could* be ignored. And another distinguished canonist, Philip Gray of the St. Joseph Foundation, made that case forcefully: "If the priest believes in his conscience — because primacy of conscience is a matter — if the priest believes there is a violation of divine law by the bishop's directive, he has an obligation to the divine law."

Whose Directives?

The problem became still more complicated if the bishop seemed simply to be relaying the orders of a secular government official. Since diocesan directives regularly followed immediately after emergency orders from mayors and governors, pastors might have been forgiven for questioning whether the missives from the chancery represented the will of the bishop or of the politician.

The problem was compounded still further when bishops issued directives without invoking their authority. Often the orders to close churches and stop public celebration of the Mass came from chancery officials, not from the bishop himself. If the bishop did issue the orders, he rarely invoked his authority to command priests' obedience. In several cases that came to my attention, priests asked their bishops: Are you commanding me under obedience? Invariably the response—usually from a chancery official again, not from the bishop personally—was ambiguous.

This second potential conflict, between priests and their bishops, reflects in this case the potential tension between Church and state. The state has a legitimate interest in protecting the physical health of the populace, but the Church has a more important purpose. As Philip Gray put it succinctly, "We're talking about the life and death of the soul."

In Poland, Archbishop Stanislaw Gadecki, the head of the nation's episcopal conference, made that point as he encouraged priests to schedule *more* public celebrations of the Mass, so that the pews would be less crowded and the likelihood of contagion diminished. "In the current situation," he said, "I wish to remind you that just as hospitals treat diseases of the body, so the Church serves to—among other things—treat illness of the soul; that is why it is unimaginable that we do not pray in our churches." Showing a flawless mathematical logic, he reasoned:

> Acknowledging the recommendation of the Chief Sanitary Inspector that there not be large gatherings of people, I'm asking for the increase—insofar as this is possible—in the number of Sunday Masses in the churches, so that at any one time the number of faithful participating in the liturgies are according to the sanitary regulation.

Accepting the Lockdown

Other bishops pushed in the opposite direction, however, going beyond the orders of public officials in shutting down their parishes. In March, Governor Mike DeWine of Ohio did not order the state's churches closed. Nevertheless, the Catholic bishops of Ohio announced that public worship would be suspended —not only for a few weeks, which at the time was the general expectation about the length of the lockdown, but through the end of May.

When May arrived, with the lockdown still in place, the bishops of the four dioceses of Iowa went still further, saying that they planned to keep restrictions on their parishes in place until "an effective vaccine" was available. This announcement came at a time when the most optimistic projections put the approval of a vaccine several months in the future. And the Iowa bishops indicated that they planned to hold to their policy, keeping a tight clampdown on parish activities, even if the state's government eased restrictions.

In Great Britain, by May the Catholic bishops had become restive about the continued tight restrictions imposed by the government on churches. But as I read a complaint issued in May by the Catholic bishops of England and Wales, I honestly could not determine whether the Church leaders were faulting the government for acting too quickly or too slowly in allowing churches to reopen. The key sentence read:

> The timing and the manner of the opening of churches touches profound sensitivities and spiritual needs. The Government's document and statements fail to recognize this.

Apparently, the bishops intended to suggest that the "profound sensitivities and spiritual needs" pointed to an earlier opening of the churches. (As things stood at the time, the government's plan called for the churches to stay closed until July 4.) But the bishops' conference, which had so carefully sidestepped confrontation, was too polite to press the issue. Instead, the bishops respectfully announced: "The Church is ready to play its full part in the task force, understanding that this includes the possible earlier use of churches for private prayer, as a first step towards their use for public worship."

Contrast that anodyne statement with the aggressive behavior of those who demanded the unconditional closing of all Catholic institutions — as in Valencia, Spain, where Cardinal Antonio Canizares was under investigation by local prosecutors for having had the temerity to open a basilica door and impart a blessing on the people standing outside. When militant secularists said that the churches should be closed, they seemed to mean it literally: that the doors of the buildings could not be opened, and sacred images could not be exposed to public view. If Church leaders had been equally energetic in asserting the rights of the Church and the lay faithful equally aggressive in defending their freedom of worship, the world at large might have been more likely to recognize the message that the Church was designed to convey: the message of the First Commandment, the message that religious worship is an essential activity.

Yet even as secular governments began to ease onerous restrictions on worship, prominent Church leaders urged the faithful to honor government regulations. In May, as Italian officials lifted a blanket ban on the public celebration of Mass, Pope Francis told a public audience:

> In some countries liturgical celebrations with the faithful have resumed; in others the possibility is being considered. In Italy, from tomorrow it will be possible to celebrate Holy Mass with the people; but please, let us

go ahead with the rules, the prescriptions they give us, so as to protect the health of each person and of the people.

Why were Church leaders so very anxious to comply with government restrictions? Again the question arises: Were bishops making a pastoral judgment that their churches should be closed, or were they bowing to the demands of government officials? The bishops had the authority to close churches, whether or not they were wise to do so. But they did *not* have the authority to bow to Caesar—to sacrifice the religious freedom of the Catholic Church and the Catholic faithful. Which were they doing?

The Obligation to Worship

In many cases, the public statements issued by Catholic bishops reinforced concerns that they were acting out of obedience to their political overseers rather than as shepherds of their flocks. In Virginia, for example, Catholic bishops issued guidelines for parishes to comply with orders issued by Governor Ralph Northam, who explained the tight constraints that he imposed on churches by making a statement that challenged Catholic faith and practice:

> Is it the worship or the building? For me, God is wherever you are. You don't have to sit in the church pew for God to hear your prayers. Worship with a mask on is still worship. Worship outside or worship online is still worship.

Yes, worship online is still worship. Yes, anyone can pray anywhere. But offering a private prayer at home is not participating in the Mass, nor is an online experience the same as a community gathering. More to the point, the governor of Virginia does not set the standards for what is or is not appropriate Catholic worship. Nevertheless, Catholic pastors in Virginia enforced the governor's standards—just as pastors around the country enforced standards set by other mayors, governors, and commissioners.

When government officials issued shutdown regulations, many bishops quickly announced that the public celebration of Mass would be suspended, without bothering to mention that the faithful would be dispensed from their obligation to attend Mass on Sunday. That obligation is a serious one, carrying the pain of mortal sin for those Catholics who skip Sunday Mass without a serious reason. Of course, there is never a moral obligation to do the impossible, and by closing down the churches, the bishops had made attendance at Sunday Mass impossible. Still, a bishop could ease consciences and eliminate confusion simply by saying that the Sunday Mass obligation would no longer apply. Many bishops did make that announcement. But many others did not, and that is telling.

While bishops have authority over the administration of the sacraments, it is questionable, at least, whether they have the authority to shut down all access to the sacraments. Yet they did. In the case of bishops who announced the closing of churches without saying anything about lifting the Sunday obligation, they were choosing to do what they arguably had no right to do, while *not* doing what they certainly *did* have the authority to do.

Could the bishops dispense their people from the obligation to attend Mass on Sunday? That is a question on which canon lawyers differ. The requirement to attend Sunday Mass is a precept of the Church, and so it would seem that the Church, through her leaders, could change or suspend it. But the obligation to "keep holy the Lord's Day" is one of the Ten Commandments, which no one has the right to alter. Cardinal Raymond Burke, one of the world's leading experts on canon law, explained in May:

The Sunday Mass obligation, for instance, participates in natural and divine law, the Third Commandment of the Decalogue, which we are obliged to observe, unless, for reasons beyond our control, we are not able to do so. During the present crisis, it has been said that bishops dispense the faithful from the Sunday Mass obligation, but no human has the power to dispense from divine law. If it has been impossible, during the crisis for the faithful to assist at Holy Mass, then the obligation did not bind them, but the obligation remained.

If the obligation remained but did not bind the faithful, then it seems that bishops took upon themselves the moral responsibility for making Sunday Mass unavailable. Still, the Third Commandment continued to apply; the faithful were required by God's clear mandate to do something—to engage in some form of prayer, preferably liturgical prayer—on Sunday. The *Catechism of the Catholic Church* (2183), quoting the Code of Canon Law, stipulates:

> If it is impossible to assist at a Eucharistic celebration, either because no sacred minister is available or for some other grave reason, the faithful are strongly recommended to take part in a liturgy of the Word... or to spend an appropriate time in prayer, whether personally or as a family or, as occasion presents, as a group of families.

The failure to emphasize the Sunday obligation is sure to have another deleterious effect that will endure long beyond the Covid shutdown. In normal times, many Catholics skip Sunday Mass, either ignorant of or indifferent to the Church's stern admonitions. Now the bishops closed down access to

Sunday Mass, in many cases without mentioning the normal obligation to attend or the enduring obligation to observe the Lord's Day in some form of prayer. (The typical directive *did* stress the importance of preserving health and safety but not the duty of Sunday worship.) By doing so, they encouraged the lax attitude of Catholics—perhaps already a majority—who think of attendance at Sunday Mass as an option, not an obligation. That attitude would not easily be changed when the churches reopen.

The lax attitude was powerfully reinforced, too, by the bishops (and other Church officials) who told the lay faithful that instead of attending Mass on Sunday, they could *watch* the Eucharistic liturgy on television on the internet. *Watching* a ceremony is not the same as *participating* in that ceremony—a distinction that I shall explore in more depth in Chapter 4. Even a hint that a livestream Mass was an acceptable substitute for the Real Presence was an affront to the faith of loyal Catholics, and for those with a less informed or less zealous faith, it was an invitation to an even more lax approach.

If the bishops, in their church-closing announcements, had given some indication that they knew how painful this step would be for the laity, their sympathy might have alleviated the pain. But most bishops, in their public statements, were too busy pretending that this was not a crisis for the Church, that liturgical life could continue unimpeded—too busy to spend any time offering consolation to those who felt abandoned.

To be sure it was true, as many diocesan bulletins pointed out, that the eucharistic liturgy would still be accomplished. Priests were instructed to continue the daily celebration of Mass—privately, in the churches they had closed off to their people. But the bulletins did not convey any sorrow over the absence of the lay faithful. On the contrary, many episcopal directives conveyed the impression that lay Catholics who were pleading to attend Mass had become a nuisance.

In May, several weeks into the lockdown, one bishop issued a video statement warning the faithful that they could not expect their churches to open again any time soon. (He made his statement wearing a mask, although there was obviously no one near him in the studio: an obvious bit of virtue-signaling.) Regular public celebration of the Mass, he said, would not resume until there were no restrictions. *No* restrictions? And *whose* restrictions? The bishop seemed to be indicating his willingness to allow government officials (which officials?) to determine when the faithful would be allowed at Mass.

In July, on the other side of the country, another bishop felt obliged to tighten restrictions on the use of his churches. Weddings and funerals would "need to be postponed," he said, until the spread of the virus was curbed. "I regret the inconvenience that these restrictions will cause," the bishop said, "but our priority must be the well-being of all our members."

The "well-being of all our members" should, in the eyes of a Catholic bishop, mean primarily their *spiritual* welfare, which is endangered by withholding the sacraments. And to "regret the inconvenience" of one's decision is to use the cold language of a bureaucrat. But there was yet another reason to raise one's eyebrows at this bishop's statement: he was taking for granted a secularized view of the church's role.

To Keep the Faith Alive

Many half-hearted Catholics look at the church as a place to hold events: weddings, funerals, or in this case (involving a heavily Hispanic diocese), *quinceañeras*. If an unserious Catholic family cannot line up the local parish for a wedding, that is indeed *inconvenient*—just as it is inconvenient if the parish hall cannot be reserved for the reception. If, on the other hand, a serious Catholic looks upon at the church as a place of prayer and solemnity and consecration, the bishop's message says nothing to him. Such statements from bishops reminded some lay Catholics of Flannery O'Connor's complaint: "It seems to be a fact that you have to suffer as much from the Church as for it."

Fortunately, not all Church leaders responded with such alacrity to government calls for a lockdown. In Texas, Bishop Joseph Strickland of Tyler had a different response to the crisis:

> I call on every Catholic priest to lead a simple Eucharistic Procession around your Church sometime before the Feast of St Joseph, March 19, for repentance, Christ's healing hand on the Coronavirus & that all men may be Godly, manly sons & disciples of His Son Jesus Christ.

In New Hampshire, Bishop Peter Libasci had the same idea. He led eucharistic processions through the streets of cities. If the people could not come to their churches to encounter their eucharistic Lord, the bishop would bring Him to the people.

Other pastors, scattered across the country, looked for inventive ways to serve their people without violating their bishop's orders. Some celebrated Mass in the parking lots of their parishes, with the "congregation" staying in their cars. Others arranged for "drive-through" confessions, allowing the faithful to obtain absolution for their sins while preserving the "social distancing" formula set by public health officials. Sadly, more than a few bishops looked askance at these efforts. In at least thirty American dioceses, drive-through confessions were explicitly banned.

Yet again, those bans conveyed a troubling message. The most diligent pastors — the priests who were determined to find ways to administer the sacraments — were seen by diocesan officials as troublemakers. Meanwhile, the pastors who were content to serve out the lockdown quietly in the comfort of their rectories won kudos from the chanceries. So energetic pastors were discouraged, and lazy priests were rewarded. Here too the negative effects of the lockdown were sure to remain even after the Covid crisis passed.

Reluctant Shepherds

As the weeks passed and some government restrictions were lifted, bishops and pastors diverged in their reactions. Some leapt to arrange for public celebration of Mass, making whatever arrangements were necessary in order to comply with official directives. Others demurred, asking for more time, saying that the safe administration of the sacraments would require weeks of preparation.

In August, public health officials in New Zealand allowed for religious ceremonies, as long as no more than one hundred people took part. But Cardinal John Dew of Wellington announced that the public celebration of Mass would not resume because it "proved very difficult" to make appropriate arrangements. He went on to instruct his priests *not* to hear confessions or take the sacraments to the sick — although he allowed that priests might "make their own decisions" about anointing those who were near death.

Many pastors can testify that indeed it "proved very difficult" to reopen churches under the newly relaxed restrictions. Diocesan officials issued long, detailed instructions on how the churches should be cleaned, pews roped off, masks worn, sanitizer dispensed. Bishops who had never worried about the proper reception of Communion now gave explicit instructions on the sanitation of the process. In short, bishops who had not previously evinced any real concern about the rubrics of the eucharistic liturgy now went into excruciating detail—in one case a sixty-three-page memo—about how the liturgy should be celebrated. After decades of neglect, which helped to cause a crisis of faith, it took a public health crisis to focus attention on liturgical guidelines. And now, when the focus finally was placed on liturgical propriety, the goal was not reverence but hygiene.

In one large American archdiocese, the manual for reopening parishes sternly underlined the need for social distancing but made this remarkable concession:

> Take into account that members of a single household may not need to remain socially distant from one another—a husband and wife and two kids could perhaps sit close to each other—so the areas you mark out should take that into account.

Surely, it was kind of archdiocesan officials to vouchsafe that a husband and wife *might* sit together. And even their *two* children could be with them. What about larger families? The archdiocesan manual was silent.

In Canada, one bishop was not ready even to make that sort of concession to family solidarity. He announced that public celebration of the Mass would still not be allowed and although weddings might be possible, he strongly recommended against them because no more than ten people would be allowed in the church. He clarified: "This must take into account everyone, musicians, pastor, wedding party, and guests. No exceptions."

And that was not all:

And, we must respect the order to continue social distancing at two meters. This would include the bride and groom. Therefore, I would suggest the wedding be postponed to a better time.

That's right: During the wedding ceremony, as they pledged to give themselves totally to each other, the bride and groom were required to preserve a decorous distance of two meters between them. The bishop, to his credit, did not require that they maintain social distancing on their wedding night.

3

The Cure Worse Than the Disease

As I write, in late October 2020, more than one million people have died of Covid, about 230,000 of them in the United States, according to official statistics. But that death toll reflects only a part of the damage that has been done by both the disease and the public reaction.

Beginning in March, the world's political leaders rushed to adopt the most extreme public policy measures ever seriously considered outside wartime, shutting down the economic and social lives of their people. Never before had national leaders deliberately taken steps that were sure to plunge their countries into deep economic recession—or worse. In March and April, they took those fateful steps, and by October they were contemplating another stiff dose of the same medicine, with more likely to come as each successive dose failed to stop the spread of a very infectious disease.

The economic costs of the lockdown have been incalculable. Since this is not a book on public policy, suffice it to say that millions of people have lost their jobs, tens of thousands of businesses have closed, education and research and development have slowed to a crawl. In a gesture intended to ease the suffering, U.S. lawmakers quickly spent $2.2 *trillion* on a "stimulus package," and by October were considering another spending bill with a similar price tag. Since the federal government is already awash in red ink, those huge figures will be added onto the enormous debt burden that future generations of Americans will be forced to carry.

Social Costs

And those are only the economic costs of the lockdown. Consider too the social costs: the damage done to families that could not — and still cannot — come together; the lost opportunities for friendship and for the blossoming of young love; the cramped outlook of children confined to their homes, unable to make new friends, experiencing the world as a frightening place where all strangers must be avoided.

All this damage has been justified, in the minds of public officials, by the urgent need to protect public health. Yet public health, too, has suffered immensely. With hospitals and clinics scaling back their services to accommodate the predicted rush of Covid patients (which in most places never materialized), other important medical procedures were postponed or skipped entirely, sometimes with deadly consequences. Cancers were not detected until they had metastasized; heart disease went unnoticed until a traumatic incident. By November, the Centers for Disease Control (CDC) estimated that there had been over 100,000 "excess deaths" in the United States during the calendar year: deaths that would not have occurred under normal circumstances. In other words, by the CDC's own account, for every two people who had died because of Covid, another American had died because of the policies designed to curb the spread of Covid. Bear in mind, too, that the "excess deaths" for 2020 will not be the only deaths attributable to the lockdown; some people will die next year, or the year after that, of cancer that might have been treated successfully if it had been detected in time.

The Covid virus emerged as a dangerous killer in 2019. But tuberculosis, the world's most deadly infectious disease, kills more than a million people worldwide—mostly in undeveloped countries—every year. The fight against tuberculosis has been set back seriously during the Covid lockdown. Because of an enormous drop in the number of people being tested for tuberculosis, experts estimate that the world will see an additional six million fatal cases over the next five years.

The Covid death toll was highest among the elderly and, particularly, those living in nursing homes and assisted-living facilities. But even in those institutions the "excess deaths" were piling up. One nurse working in a long-term care facility reported that her patients were dying primarily from "failure to thrive." They were losing the will to live, facing the bleak prospect of month after month without relief, without visits from loved ones, without recreation, with their only human contact coming from workers who wore masks and gloves and avoided touching them whenever possible. They were, in short, dying of loneliness.

Pregnant women suffered, too, as routine check-ups were scaled back and possible complications went undiagnosed. The rate of infant mortality jumped. Mothers were forced to give birth without the support of their husbands because hospital policies barred all "nonessential" personnel from the ward. Newborn infants were whisked away from their mothers by nurses who made the inhuman judgment that the mother was a threat to her baby's health. The *Manchester Guardian* remarked:

> [Pregnant women were] unable to have a birth com-
> panion, coerced into undergoing medical interventions,

denied pain relief, and separated from their newborns. This is the new reality for expectant and new mothers in the many countries, as experts warn the coronavirus outbreak is leading to an infringement of women's birth rights.

An "infringement of women's birth rights" would not show up on CDC statistics about public health. Nor would the trauma and the anger of the mothers separated from their children or the fathers denied the chance to hold their newborn children. (Bear in mind that they were kept away from *their* children by representatives of the state or the medical establishment, who had usurped the role of primary caregivers.)

The lockdown caused special problems for those who were already suffering from emotional difficulties—and added to their number by ramping up tension, frustration, and alienation felt by the millions of people sitting at home with nothing to do but worry about their future. The emotional stress had evident consequences. Deaths in the United Sates attributed to drug overdoses leapt in 2020, running about 13 percent above the figures from the previous year. Reports of domestic abuse leapt, even though, with households living in isolation, there were fewer opportunities for outsiders to spot abusive treatment.

All Deaths Are Tragedies

Mental health professionals tell us that loneliness can be quite literally deadly to someone struggling with addiction or depression or despair. Left to itself, the mind wanders through its darkest passages; the imagination conjures up problems that do not really exist. The best antidote to this unhealthy tendency is personal contact: the company of friends who can bring a troubled soul back to reality. Programs like Alcoholics Anonymous rely on this proven truth, putting vulnerable people in regular contact with others who are ready and willing to help them work through their difficulties. But those groups found it more difficult to arrange meetings during the lockdown. Even the regular routine of daily work can help someone maintain a shaky grip on reality and avoid frightening flights of the imagination. During the lockdown, however, hundreds of thousands of fragile people were thrown off their regular work routine.

Suicides soared as the lockdown left troubled people in isolation, with more than 130 Americans taking their own lives on an average day. Suicide help lines were jammed with calls; suicide became the second-leading cause of death among young Americans.

Notice, now, that if there were 100,000 "excess deaths" in 2020 not attributable to Covid, along with 80,000 drug-overdose deaths and 48,000 suicides, those figures combined begin to compare with the total number of Covid fatalities. No doubt some of those suicides and drug overdoses would have occurred even without the lockdown. On the other hand, it is not unreasonable to expect that some people who became despondent or addicted during the lockdown will turn up on the casualty list in 2021 or 2022, and their deaths will be at least partially attributable to the lockdown of 2020. Much more certainly, in those future years there will be "excess deaths" caused by cancers that might have been treated successfully if they had been detected in 2020.

So even purely from the perspective of physical health, it is quite possible that the lockdown of 2020 has done more harm than good—that the proposed cure (which actually did *not* effect a cure) has been worse than the disease. Add in the mental and emotional and spiritual health of the populace, and the balance shifts decisively against the lockdown.

The Poor Bear the Burden

As with nearly every social ill, the costs of the lockdown have been borne disproportionately by the vulnerable. Poor people are more likely to live in crowded apartment buildings, where heating and air-conditioning systems circulate the same air through different family residences, where an airborne virus can ride up and down shared elevators and float across shared hallways. The poor are more likely to commute in stuffy buses or subway cars. They are more likely to work at jobs that require constant contact with the public.

During the peak of the lockdown, most American professionals were able to continue their work from home, telecommuting from the comfort of their dens, taking extra precautions only when they left the house. A few steps down the socioeconomic ladder, however, workers in grocery stores or on factory floors had to don masks when they left home early in the morning and leave them on until they came home at night. Blue-collar workers were obliged to follow special Covid-era rules laid down by their corporate superiors, while the professionals working at home made up their own rules to fit their own convenience.

Sure enough, during the lockdown wealthy Americans prospered, enduring only an occasional small inconvenience, while the middle class suffered. Thousands of small shops were shuttered and thousands of restaurants closed, many of them permanently. A large corporation or a wealthy individual can survive for a month or two with closed doors and no income; a small mom-and-pop operation cannot. How many American families lost the equity that they had built up for generations in a small business? The costs in these cases have not only been economic; they have involved serious blows to the pride, the self-reliance, the history of working families.

Two Sets of Rules

The pains suffered by the powerless have been aggravated by the blatantly hypocritical behavior of political leaders who flouted their own lockdown orders:

- The mayor of New York who, having ruled that gyms were nonessential and must be closed, went for one last workout at his own gym.
- The Speaker of the U.S. House of Representatives, who arranged for private hair treatment at a salon that had been officially closed down.
- The mayor of Chicago who explained that hair salons were not essential, but her own visit to a salon *was* essential because "I'm the public face of this city."
- The mayor of Denver who told residents not to travel for Thanksgiving—even as he boarded a cross-country flight to visit his daughter.
- The governor of California who banned indoor public gatherings, then went out with a large group of friends for a long and noisy dinner at an expensive restaurant.

Even apart from such grotesquely selfish displays, the wealthy and powerful—the people who set public policies and guide public opinion to favor the lockdown—have, as a rule, suffered least from the effects. They have been able to do their work from home offices, conducting meetings by Zoom and Skype, practicing "social distancing" without much additional cost to themselves or their professional work. Not so the grocery store workers on whom they rely, the delivery-van drivers who bring goods to their front doors, the utility workers who keep their internet lines running. All these people are required to don a mask early in the morning and leave it in place all day (or face penalties). Lower down on the socioeconomic scale, the costs of the lockdown have been greater, the opportunity to influence public policy less.

Writing for *The American Conservative*, Tony Woodlief gave voice to the complaint:

> The scorners can hide in their homes because my people make their world work. My people are the ones who fit the pipes that keep natural gas coming into their houses. My people are the ones who empty their septic tanks, patch their roofs, fix their cars, truck their groceries, and deliver their packages. My people are the ones who police the streets and man the barracks and douse fires after riots. If you think a country can stay home until the virus is erased, you know nothing about what and who makes your country run.

The Catholic Church, especially since the Second Vatican Council, has proclaimed a "preferential option for the poor" —that is, a determination to pay attention first and foremost to the needs of people who are most in need of help. During 2020, the preferential option should have prompted sympathy for the millions of people suffering from the effects of the lockdown, as well as the thousands suffering from the disease.

The Special Suffering of the Elderly

In the overlap between those two groups—the people suffering from Covid and the people suffering from the lockdown—the elderly were vastly overrepresented. Those living in nursing homes and assisted-living facilities were suddenly isolated: unable to receive visitors, unable to leave, effectively imprisoned for months. When public officials ordered Covid patients into those facilities, they also became incubators for a disease which, while only mildly dangerous for younger people, was deadly for the aged. The virus was the Grim Reaper of nursing homes; tens of thousands of elderly people died—and died alone. For aged men and women, longing for human contact, suffering from dementia, unable to understand the lockdown rules, wondering why their children and grandchildren did not visit them, it was a horrible death. Perhaps they were dying anyway; perhaps the Covid diagnosis was only a formality for the elderly people slowly succumbing to cancer or heart disease. They would have died in 2020 in any case. But were it not for the cruelty of the lockdown, they would not have died alone.

And some might not have died. Some did not *seem* to be in any imminent danger of death but lost their will to live in such a depressing environment and wasted away.

Other elderly people, perfectly aware of the dangers of the virus, might have chosen—if they were offered any choice—to risk the disease rather than a safe but sterile life in their institutions. One British clinician, Dr. Matt Strauss, testified in *The Spectator* of London:

> I am a life-support specialist. At this point in my career, hundreds of elderly patients have instructed me not to put them on life support. Many have told me they are comfortable with their mortality and that if not much time is left to them, they would rather spend it eating ice cream or listening to music with their family, not hooked up to my machines.

Sadly, many elderly people were not given the choice to live their last days with their family members, in the comfort and relative safety of their (or their children's) homes. They could not obtain permission to move out of institutions. They were, again, prisoners of an inflexible system. Instead of the familiar faces of their children, they saw only the staff members of the institutions. Those staff members went home to *their* own families after their shifts, so despite all precautions, there was still a risk that they would bring the virus into the nursing homes — or more likely spread it from room to room, since the virus was already haunting the facilities. A quiet room in an ordinary family home, with minimal contact from nonrelatives, could have been a safer alternative, if only it had been an option.

Young People Left Behind

The elderly were not the only people confined to institutions and subjected to inhuman regulations that reflected an unbalanced fear of the virus. In maternity wards, young mothers were told that they could not spend time with their newborn infants — after they had given birth (wearing mandatory masks all through labor) without the support of their husbands, who were kept away "for safety's sake." Older children who were hospitalized for other reasons were separated from their parents. In one particularly callous policy decision, administrators at York University in England told students who were Covid-positive that if a fire alarm sounded, they should stay in their rooms for at least a full minute so that they would not infect other students. (The stunned reaction forced administrators to rescind that policy.)

Think too of the young lovers whose marriage plans were put on hold indefinitely because of restrictions on travel and on gatherings. Think of the couples earlier on in their courtship, stuck in their own homes, unable to see the ones with whom they have fallen in love. Many weddings were postponed because of Covid; others may never happen. Who knows how many couples are living together today without the benefit of a sacramental bond because their pastors would not allow them a church wedding?

Or think of the young people starting out in their careers, finding their paths to success blocked: unable to find work because businesses were dormant, unable to find roommates because they could not meet other young people, unable to do the normal socialization that is a crucial part of becoming an adult. How many young people were forced to forfeit once-in-a-lifetime opportunities: for a year abroad, a fellowship, an athletic competition for which they had been training? Anyone aspiring to a career as a performer—a musician, an entertainer, a comedian—was stymied, since theaters and clubs were shut down. The performing arts were robbed of live audiences, and our culture was poorer for it.

Somehow—I am at a loss to explain it—the most popular forms of mass entertainment escaped the worst effects of the lockdown. Hollywood continued to grind out its glitzy products. Television sitcoms aired new episodes—in which the actors were not wearing masks nor observing social distancing. Professional sports leagues paused but then continued, the teams competing in empty arenas for television audiences.

School-age children were generally safe from this mysterious disease. But they paid a high price, too: confined to their homes, unable to play with their friends. Or they wore masks all day at primary schools and day-care centers, separated from their classmates by Plexiglas shields. They interacted with adults who wore masks, so that they could not learn to read the cues of facial expressions. How could children in the earliest grades be expected to learn how to read — to sound out letters and words — without being able to see the teacher's mouth? The world of the young child in school seemed to be inhabited exclusively by strange people who encouraged them to be frightened of human contact. Every adult knew that this situation was unusual; but for a child stepping out into the wider world for the first time, this anomic situation was the only experience of social interaction that he could know. How many nightmares were born of these situations? How many children were stunted in their socialization and emotional growth?

Writing in November in the *New York Times*, Drs. Donna Farber and Thomas Connors weighed the implications of this novel problem:

> We may also be conducting an unwitting experiment on the psychological development of our children. Living in a world of masked faces, are they learning to pick up the emotional signals that ordinarily come from facial expressions: the smiles, frowns, grimaces, and gapes that are shown mostly in the mouth? We adults learned how to recognize those cues long ago. Will our children lag?

Or for that matter, what about the negative effects on the development of children's immune systems? Wearing a face mask means depriving one's immune system of its regular daily workouts. That may be a minor issue for adults, who over the years have developed immunities to all sorts of minor airborne maladies. But young children are in a different situation; their immune systems are still developing. For them, wearing masks for the better part of a year might mean missing the chance to develop immunity to some diseases.

Families under Siege

Families suffered, too, from being unexpectedly confined to their quarters. The steady strain of living in close contact all day, every day, revealed tensions within households. While some families enjoyed their time together and drew closer, others were not so successful in coping with the extra hours at home, as the rising reports of domestic abuse illustrated.

Since different households took different attitudes toward the Covid risk, the lockdown put new strains on extended families. Some fearful grandparents announced that their children or grandchildren would not be welcome to visit because they might bring the virus with them. Even for happy families, the long gaps between visits — made necessary because of the restraints on travel — created unwonted emotional distance. When extended families came together for holidays or important family occasions, the different attitudes toward masks and tests and quarantines provided another potential source of conflict, along with the time-honored disputes about politics and religion.

Throughout this chapter, I have been using the past tense in writing about the consequences of the lockdown. But those negative consequences are still piling up, as time passes, and political leaders continue to tighten their emergency regulations. There is no end in sight; government officials suggest that Americans may be wearing masks and keeping their distance from each other — in other words, giving up all normal social interaction — for months or even possibly years to come. The cumulative effects of an extended lockdown are, by orders of magnitude, more deleterious to families and to societies than the two-week effort to "flatten the curve" that was originally proposed.

Politics, Religion, and Covid

Perhaps I was wrong to add arguments about Covid to the traditional list of dangerous topics for dinner-table conversation. It might be more accurate to say that the debates about Covid and the lockdown really *were* disputes about politics and religion, because they reflected some fundamental differences about the purposes of public policy and the meaning of human life. Humans are social animals. We are made to live in society, to interact with our family members, our friends, our neighbors. To avoid interaction is to work against our very nature. To see other people—*all* other people—as threats is perverse, an insult to the emotional and spiritual hard-wiring of the human person. The lockdown, along with the constant messages that are pounded by the media into our consciousness, encouraging us to live in isolation and to fear closeness with others, have produced the sort of dystopian environment that Thomas Hobbes sketched as the basis for his *Leviathan*: a society that sees human existence as a war of all against all, sees lives as "nasty, poor, brutish, and short."

Needless to say, this perspective is at odds with Christian thought and doctrine. The loss of community is a loss of solidarity, a loss of charity, a loss of apostolic opportunity for evangelization. Worse, the lockdown and the closing of churches meant that lay Catholics were deprived of the sacraments, the wellsprings of sanctifying grace. The Church, obedient to divine command, sees communal worship not merely as a useful and salutary thing but as a moral obligation. We do not worship *only* because we want to do so; we worship also because were required to do so, as a matter of justice. Yet for months we, as parish communities, let that fundamental obligation slide. And the end—the restoration of normal community worship—is not yet in sight.

The Covid epidemic was, without question, a serious problem, a dangerous public health emergency. But the lockdown was an intemperate, disproportionate response. The costs of the lockdown have been greater than the toll of the virus; the cure has been worse than the disease.

Speaking in August at a Napa Institute conference, Bishop Thomas Paprocki of Springfield, Illinois put the matter in a distinctively Catholic perspective. He reminded his audience that the Church has always argued that it is not morally necessary—and in some cases it may be morally wrong—to use "extraordinary means" in the fight against illness. Ordinarily the question of "extraordinary means" arises in end-of-life care: for instance, when radical surgery is proposed for a patient who is likely to die soon after the procedure or when costly or invasive intervention is suggested to prolong the life of a terminal patient for a few more days. But Bishop Paprocki reasoned that the same moral analysis could be applied to a pandemic and to the costly measures associated with the lockdown:

> Do we have a moral obligation to shut down our society, require people to stay at home, put employees out of work, send businesses into bankruptcy, impair the food supply chain, and prevent worshippers from going to church? I would say not. That would be imposing unduly burdensome and extraordinary means. While some people may voluntarily adopt such means, only ordinary means that are not unduly burdensome are morally required to preserve life both on the part of individuals as well as society as a whole.

Life always involves some degree of risk, and always—even with the best of medical care and the best of public health policy—ends in death. Adults make their own choices, weighing the risks against the benefits. To turn over all those choices to the authority of the state is to surrender the moral autonomy of adulthood. Christianity is a faith for adults.

Adults, especially adult Christians, recognize that life on this earth is not our ultimate destiny nor our ultimate goal. We are all mortal; we shall all die. While we uphold the right to life for every human being, we do not and cannot pretend that anyone has the "right" to be preserved forever from death by natural causes. We can and do fight against disease. But when the crusade against one disease becomes the medical equivalent of a scorched-earth military campaign, with costs greater than the toll of the disease itself, responsible adults should recognize that the disproportionate response is immoral.

4

The Virtual Church

"By staying home, we're saving lives." How many times was that logic invoked during the year 2020? Let's take a closer look at it.

If you know or even suspect that you have a highly infectious and potentially deadly disease, then of course, you should stay home; if you're out and about, you're putting others at risk. Quarantining the sick is a venerable public health response to the outbreak of an infectious disease. But what if there's no reason to suspect that you *are* infected with the disease? What if 99 percent of the people who do catch the disease survive it — in most cases, without serious symptoms? What if — as some of the latest available studies show, as I write — there is no compelling evidence that people who are not suffering from the symptoms of Covid can pass along the disease? In that case, when a productive citizen stays home, there's a cost to society — a cost that can ultimately be measured in lives.

In *The Price of Panic*, three authors — Douglas Axe, William Brigg, and Jay Richards — try to put the Covid epidemic in perspective. The authors do not downplay the dangers of Covid. They simply weigh those dangers against the undoubted costs of the draconian measures with which public officials have responded. They contend:

This virus triggered panic long before it compared to any other global catastrophe.... Never before had scores of countries around the world chosen to perform such economic harikari in unison.

That is a bold appraisal: one virtually guaranteed to ensure that *The Price of Panic* is not reviewed—not even mentioned—by mainstream media outlets. From the time when the lockdowns began in March, media outlets competed with each other to run the most sensational headlines about the rise in case counts, the most frightening stories about potential fatalities, the most exaggerated accounts of hospital overcrowding. Bad news sells, and Covid provided editors with a bonanza of bad news. It's clickbait. It's panic-porn. It's obsessive.

The social media giants, Facebook and Twitter and YouTube, did their part to fan the flames, suppressing questions about the alarmist narrative. This was done, the gatekeepers of the internet inform us, because it was responsible to suppress dissent in this case, because by stressing the urgency of the situation, they were saving lives. We were thus back to the logic with which I opened this chapter: We're doing these things to save lives, and that end justifies the means.

But were we locking down to save lives? That question could mean either of two things: Were we *motivated* by the desire to save lives? Were we *actually* saving lives?

Concentration of Power

Were public officials, when they ordered ever-stricter lockdown measures, motivated entirely by the desire to save lives? A reasonably prudent observer should notice that the lockdowns concentrated power in the hands of a few officials. The governor decides when an emergency exists; the governor decides what citizens should do during an emergency; the governor decides when (if ever) the emergency ends. The governor, in short, had an awful lot of power, as long as the epidemic remains a deciding factor in public opinion. How many politicians, having tasted power, want to renounce it?

For that matter, how many politicians, having ordered drastic public policies, will want to admit that they have failed? The lockdown policies were ordered by governors and mayors on the basis of suggestions from public health officials. Could we reasonably expect those public health officials and/or those elected politicians to admit that they chose wrongly?

The lockdown began because public health officials predicted an unprecedented disaster. We shall never know what might have happened if our political leaders had declined to impose harsh restrictions on society (although we might look to Sweden and learn some interesting lessons). But we do know that the "expert" predictions were consistently wrong. The authors of *The Price of Panic* observed that under some circumstances — such as the ones prevailing today — prophets pay no penalty for inaccurate predictions:

> Elijah predicted a drought.... However right he was, no one wanted to hear what Elijah had to say. No one thanked him when the prophesied drought came to pass....
>
> Being wrong in the right direction, though, often reaps reward. Early pandemic models indicated that only prompt and massive state action could save us. The models were wrong — way off — but they were wrong in the right direction. They gave politicians justification for

taking over almost every aspect of citizens' lives. They gave the press clickbait galore.

The constant drive to accentuate the negative—the competition to provide bad news—discouraged the sort of "wait a minute" skepticism that might have made the "experts" uneasy and led political leaders to hesitate about following their advice. Early in 2019, the World Health Organization (WHO) was advising that "non-pharmaceutical public health measures" like lockdowns and social distancing and masks and contact tracing would have "limited" use in fighting a flu-type epidemic. As recently as February—just a few weeks before the lockdowns began—the Surgeon General of the United States tweeted: "Seriously, people—STOP BUYING MASKS! They are NOT effective in preventing general public from catching #coronavirus, but if healthcare providers can't get them to care for sick patients, it puts them and our communities at risk!"

Those advisories were soon "inoperative," to use a term made famous by the embattled Nixon White House. But the lockdowns continued. And when lockdowns and testing failed to stop the spread of the virus, officials ordered tighter lockdowns and more testing. To step back just for a moment and ask about the effectiveness of these measures was to risk public censure. But a few intrepid researchers took that risk and made a remarkable discovery: the pattern of spreading Covid infection appeared to be the same—across different American states, across different countries—whether there were lockdowns and mask mandates and contact tracing or not. Government policies had no apparent effect on the disease.

So there really was no evidence that lockdowns were saving lives. There was abundant evidence, on the other hand, that the lockdowns imposed immense costs on society.

Defining What Is Essential

The lockdowns were never complete, of course. They could not be. People need food, medicines and medical care, heat and light and shelter. So the government officials who declared the lockdowns were forced to list the "essential" businesses that could continue operating on a more or less normal basis. The results were often revealing, sometimes comical.

Grocery stores were deemed essential, naturally. Liquor stores were, too: a decision that was easy to understand—no one wanted to cope with the outrage of citizens denied their nightly happy hours—but not so easy to explain logically. Pharmacies were essential, as were gas stations and auto-repair shops. Government agencies were very reluctant to declare *themselves* inessential, although most bureaucrats were able to work from their homes.

The logic-chopping involved in preparing a list of "essential" businesses drove some public officials to absurd lengths. Many stores had both "essential" and "nonessential" components. In some jurisdictions, hardware stores were allowed to sell tools but not seeds—although it would seem clearly beneficial, in a time of crisis, for homeowners to grow their own vegetables. Big-box stores were directed to close down some sections, putting the toys and electronic gadgets off limits, allowing customers to buy only food and household staples—although it was not easy to understand why, once he was inside Costco, a customer would be more vulnerable to infection if he bought a new VCR than if he stocked up on toilet paper.

In any event, "nonessential" institutions were subject to strict controls, imposed by bureaucrats who may or may not have understood the workings of those institutions. And in one American state after another, governors decided that churches were not essential. So churches were subject to emergency guidelines that dictated when they could be open, how long their services could last, how many people could attend, and — most intrusive of all — what could be done during worship services.

Pastors Acquiesce

Why did leaders of the Catholic Church accept this government intrusion? There were protests, to be sure, with clerics insisting that the work of the Church *was* essential. But few pastors dared to remind the faithful that the Ten Commandments carry greater authority than a governor's emergency orders. A handful of lawsuits were filed to challenge the restrictions on public worship, with small Protestant denominations as plaintiffs, joined by only a few Catholic priests. Not one American Catholic bishop even hinted at open resistance against the restrictions.

Maybe Catholic prelates were anxious to avoid confrontations with political leaders because they had come to rely so heavily on government funding for their charitable agencies. Or maybe they shied away from the negative publicity that such a confrontation would bring because the Church had been so badly scarred by the fallout from the sex-abuse scandal. Whatever the reason, one bishop after another insisted that he, not the local political powers, had made the decision to close down churches. In Massachusetts, when one resident filed a lawsuit, charging that the state government had denied him access to the Eucharist, the state's lawyers could very reasonably respond that it was not the state, but the Church, that denied him.

Having made the claim that *they* were closing the churches, out of fear of spreading the virus, bishops were in a poor position to complain about the specific rules issued by political authorities — even if they were onerous, even if they were absurd. So the rules quickly multiplied: only twenty people could be in a church at one time, regardless of the size of the church; or only fifty; or only one visitor at a time for private prayer. In Scotland, one angry priest, Father Stephen Dunn, reported that a family had traveled fifteen miles to visit a church in Glasgow, only to be turned away at the door because there were already fifty people—the government-ordered maximum—inside, and there would be no flexibility whatsoever in the observance of that government mandate.

The same sort of strict and inflexible rules applied to the work of Catholic chaplains in hospitals, and again Church leaders were punctilious in their observance. "Priests and chaplains must follow the visiting instructions from Hospital and Trust authorities," wrote Bishop Paul Mason, representing the Catholic Bishops' Conference of England and Wales. In practice, those instructions required chaplains to confer with hospital officials before visiting the sick and, in most cases, to arrange for "telephone support" of Covid patients rather than actually meeting with them and conferring the sacraments. Bishop Mason told the chaplains: "Whilst this runs counter to our instinct to provide end-of-life sacramental and pastoral care, in the current circumstances minimizing the spread of the virus must be the priority of all."

Surely minimizing the spread of the virus should have been *a* priority—a very high priority—for anyone working at a health care institution. But if it had become *the* priority for clerics associated with the hospitals, then those clerics had ceased to act primarily as priests. The decision to give physical health priority over spiritual health was an inversion of the chaplain's purpose.

Protestant Resistance

Oddly enough, although the Catholic Church insists on the necessity of physical presence for the sacraments, it was Protestant churches—usually small Evangelical churches—that bridled against the government restrictions. In Worcester, Massachusetts, Pastor Kristopher Casey of Adams Square Baptist Church announced: "We're having church because church is essential." He added, "You can't baptize someone in a Zoom meeting." His defiance drew several squad cars to Adams Square, and Pastor Casey was soon facing criminal charges.

Carl Schmitt, the lawyer who represented Pastor Casey in court, argued that the state's guidelines, which placed special restrictions on houses of worship, were an undue and unconstitutional burden on religious freedom. Schmitt found state officials anxious to settle the case, probably because they realized that their guidelines had been drawn up in haste, without any consultation with pastors and without any serious constitutional analysis. "Nothing focuses one's attention like a date with a federal judge," Schmitt observed, and within a matter of days the guidelines had been rewritten to allow religious services to proceed, with reasonable precautions in place.

In California, a much larger church, the Grace Community Church led by Pastor John MacArthur also defied government guidelines—and joined in a public relations battle with officials of Los Angeles County. When public officials called attention to three members of the Grace congregation who had tested positive for the coronavirus, an attorney for the church shot back: "Three very mild positive tests among more than 7,000 people is hardly news. 0.0004% is not an 'outbreak.'" The attorney continued:

Our position has been that LA County shutting down churches indefinitely amid a virus with a 99.98 percent survival rate, especially when state-preferred businesses are open and protests are held without restriction, is unconstitutional and harmful to the free exercise of religion.

These Protestant churches could test the guidelines in court because they were in "legal jeopardy"—that is, they faced criminal or civil charges, or both. Schmitt explained to me that American courts are usually reluctant to hear the case of a plaintiff who wants to challenge a law or policy that *might* harm him; the case is ripe for judgment when the plaintiff has actually violated the law or policy and faces charges. No Catholic church had defied the law, thus no Catholic church was in legal jeopardy, and no Catholic church had solid standing as a potential plaintiff to challenge the restrictions.

Federal Interventions

While Catholic bishops chose not to challenge restraints on the sacramental life of the Church, the Trump administration eventually stepped in to take action. In October, the Department of Health and Human Services forced two hospitals, in Maryland and Virginia, to amend policies that had prevented Catholic priests from ministering to patients. The Department's Office of Civil Rights reminded hospital administrators that federal law requires health care facilities to "ensure patients have adequate and lawful access to chaplains or clergy in conformance with the Religious Freedom Restoration Act." Before that intervention by federal officials, one hospital had refused to allow the baptism of a newborn baby, while the other had declined to allow a priest to administer the last rites to a dying Covid patient.

The restrictions on religious ceremonies—at times written with every evidence of slapdash haste, at other times crafted with meticulous attention to petty detail—produced some comical results. More than a few Facebook users wryly commented that since large stores were allowed more occupants than large churches, the next Sunday's worship services should be held in the produce section at Walmart.

In a New England city, a Catholic priest visited a hospital—carefully complying with all the institutional protocols—and volunteered to bring the sacraments to patients in the Covid ward. At first the administration resisted, fearful that he would be exposed to the virus. He explained that he had already been exposed; he lived in a home with several other priests, one of whom had been hospitalized with the disease; he had tested positive for the virus himself, quarantined for two weeks, and then tested negative; he now considered himself immune. But upon hearing this tale, the hospital administrators not only barred him from the Covid ward—on the curious theory that he might spread the virus among people already infected—but in fact must leave the hospital immediately. His positive test, even though it was safely in the past, and even though he had more recently tested negative, made him persona non grata.

Another priest, in the Boston archdiocese, had more success entering Covid wards. Father Ryan Connors joined a special cadre of priests who volunteered for the duty. Heavily armed with personal protective equipment, these brave priests took turns bringing the sacraments to the sick and dying, then returned to the home that they shared and isolated themselves, lest they somehow, despite all the care they took, bring the virus home with them. Father Connors told the *New York Times* that Catholic priests had always brought the sacraments to the sick and dying, even at peril to their own health, during epidemics, and always would do the same in the future. "In four hundred years, whatever happens in a pandemic, there will be priests to anoint God's people," he said.

Sadly, that attitude was not universal among the Catholic clergy. As the summer of 2020 brought an easing of fears about Covid, public officials lifted some restrictions on religious institutions. Catholic churches were allowed to open for Mass, provided that they held the size of their congregations to a fraction of their church's normal capacity and took various steps to ensure social distancing and frequent disinfecting of all surfaces. Some pastors leapt at the opportunity, making their churches ready to open as soon as possible. Others held back, saying that it would take weeks to comply with all the requirements of the new directives.

In another New England city, one priest—who was waiting out the lockdown at his summer home on Cape Cod—said that he could not possibly comply with the new requirements in time to open his church when the new directives went into effect. It would take much longer than two weeks, he explained, to wipe down seats, tape off every other pew, and remove hymnals from the church. So—rather than recruiting parishioners to help with the work, which could have been done in a few hours by a large crew—he remained at his vacation home. His lackadaisical attitude was, alas, not unique. Many priests, with the apparent approval of their bishops, assured the faithful that they would not reopen their churches until it was safe to do so. How safe? That question was never answered.

In some cases, bishops set out such a long list of precautionary measures and required so many different hygienic procedures that a small parish simply could not comply. If the church was too small to allow separate one-way aisles and exits, or if the prescribed sanitation process required more hands than the parish staff could furnish, there was no option but to close down the little church.

But even while they kept their parish churches closed, pastors repeatedly asked their people to continue sending in their regular weekly donations. The parish still had bills to pay, they remarked, even if there were no services rendered. Online giving was especially encouraged, since it involved no risk of contamination.

Virtual Worship

To a remarkable extent, in fact, parish life had shifted to the internet. Priests celebrated Mass in their churches without congregations but with a video camera set up so that the eucharistic sacrifice could be broadcast or, more commonly, livestreamed. Anxious to reassure the faithful that they were not estranged from the church, priests told them that they could participate online in the Mass in the safety of their homes.

But watching a livestreamed Mass is not the same as attending Mass in person. At best, a broadcast is a poor substitute for the reality. It is true that a devout Catholic could, as priests regularly recommended, make a "spiritual communion" while watching the livestream Mass. But St. Alphonsus Liguori, a great advocate of spiritual communions, emphasized that this practice was not a substitute for the actual reception of the Eucharist. A spiritual communion, he said, always anticipates the actual reception of the Body and Blood of Christ. The prayer recommended by St. Alphonsus makes this clear: "Since I cannot now receive You sacramentally, come at least spiritually into my heart."

The sacraments of the Catholic Church always involve real, concrete matter: the water of baptism, the oils of anointing in confirmation and ordination, the bread and wine offered at Mass. When the faithful attend Mass, they are participating in the Sacrifice of Calvary. When they watch it online, they are—watching, from a distance.

If a Catholic can *watch* the Mass from his home, why should he watch the livestreamed liturgy from his own parish, when another church might offer better production values? Why should he watch on Sunday at 10:30 a.m., if he could play the same video at a time more convenient to his own schedule? So the Catholic at home is no longer part of a communal gathering.

Watching a Mass online—at home, in the kitchen—also creates unique opportunities for distraction. The computer in the den does not provide a sacred space, like a church designed to encourage prayerful reflection. Journalist Sohrab Ahmari, a convert to Catholicism, was candid about the ungodly distractions that he had to fight:

> Worse, I find my fingers hovering, twitching, tingling over my smartphone, before eventually giving in and grabbing the damned thing, to catch up on my latest feuds with strangers on Twitter. Worse still—Lord, forgive me!—I've had to stop myself from pouring a glass of wine or grabbing some crisps in the middle of Internet Mass, because that's what I normally do when I watch shows on my laptop.

Sadly, a Catholic who becomes accustomed to the livestream Mass can lose his appreciation for the Real Presence of Jesus in the Eucharist. He is, after all, experiencing only what one priest termed "the virtual presence." He is seeing pixels on a screen: an image, not an immediate reality.

Remote Preparation for Remote Worship

To be fair, the move to livestreamed Mass—which would surely have been unthinkable to Catholics a generation or two ago — may have been more acceptable to Catholics of the current day because for the past few decades, at massive worldwide gatherings such as World Youth Day, hundreds of thousands of people have assembled for eucharistic liturgies celebrated by Popes John Paul II, Benedict XVI, and Francis. With a congregation of such unwieldy size, many thousands of people have been able only to watch the Pope on a video screen, stretching the understanding of a "congregation" to the breaking point.

Most Catholic bishops encouraged the faithful be docile, to accept the livestreamed Mass as a substitute for communal worship. But just a few short months earlier, when the worldwide Synod of Bishops met to discuss the difficulties of the Church in the Amazon region, liberal bishops were lobbying energetically for a relaxation of clerical celibacy, arguing that amid a critical shortage of priests in that region, it was absolutely essential for the faithful to have immediate access to the Eucharist. How was it, then, less essential for the faithful to have immediate access to the Eucharist in parishes where priests were available?

Bishops also piously assured the faithful that the Mass was still being celebrated: by their priests, behind the locked doors of their parish churches. But this, too, involved a sharp break from the familiar argument that a priest should not ordinarily celebrate Mass without a congregation. Granted, the Covid epidemic produced extraordinary circumstances. Still, the Church has always cautioned that the Mass should be celebrated for the people.

The Council of Trent taught (in Canon 528.2):

> The parish priest is to take care that the blessed Eucharist
> is the center of the parish assembly of the faithful. He is
> to strive to ensure that the faithful are nourished by the
> devout celebration of the sacraments and, in particular,

that they frequently approach the sacraments of the blessed Eucharist and penance. He is to strive to lead them to prayer, including prayer in their families, and to take a live and active part in the sacred liturgy.

The current *Code of Canon Law* (#906) echoes that message, stipulating: "A priest may not celebrate the Eucharistic Sacrifice without the participation of at least one of the faithful, unless there is a good and reasonable cause for doing so." And when pastors told parishioners that they could not join in the Eucharist, they were at least testing the bounds of Canon 912, which reads: "Any baptized person who is not forbidden by law may and must be admitted to holy Communion."

Many priests succumbed to the temptation to skip the regular celebration of the Mass — in effect outsourcing their responsibility to other priests. In a parish whose church was closed to the public, if one priest was unlocking the building each morning to celebrate a livestream Mass, others did not feel the obligation to say Mass themselves.

Chafing at the restrictions that kept them locked out of their parish churches, longing for the Mass and the Eucharist, faithful Catholics looked to their Church leaders for help. Instead, they found their bishops sternly admonishing them to obey the rules, to submit to the restrictions, to accept the loss of the sacraments.

In June, speaking to health care workers in Italy's Lombardy region, Pope Francis decried the "adolescent" complaints of Catholics who objected to church closings. He went further in a conversation with journalist Austen Ivereigh, published in book form as *Let Us Dream: The Path to a Better Future*. There the pontiff scoffed at "those who claim, for example, that being forced to wear a mask is an unwarranted imposition by the state, yet who forget or do not care about those who cannot rely, for example, on social security or who have lost their jobs."

Personally, I have not encountered a single person who objected to the mask mandate who did not also worry about people who lost their jobs in the lockdown. In fact, had he thought before he spoke, the pope should have realized that the people who question the mask mandate are the same people who object to the government policies that destroy jobs — while he, by advising docile support for the lockdown, was contributing to the loss of jobs!

Pope John Paul II, speaking in 1979, had given a very different perspective on the longing of the faithful for the Eucharist:

> Think of the places where people anxiously await a priest, and where for many years, feeling the lack of such a priest, they do not cease to hope for his presence. And sometimes it happens that they meet in an abandoned shrine, and place on the altar a stole which they still keep, and recite all the prayers of the Eucharistic liturgy; and then, at the moment that corresponds to the transubstantiation a deep silence comes down upon them, a silence sometimes broken by a sob... so ardently do they desire to hear the words that only the lips of a priest can efficaciously utter. So much do they desire Eucharistic Communion, in which they can share only through the ministry of a priest.

In 2020, the priests were available. But tragically, they were not celebrating Mass with their people. The Church was not suffering persecution (at least not in the Western world), yet the sacraments were not available.

In Ireland, the Covid lockdown of 2020 produced an eerie result. Faithful lay Catholics began to gather at the "Mass Rocks" where, beginning in the sixteenth century, the Catholic faith had been bitterly repressed for generations and brave bands of Catholics had congregated secretly for Mass. They could not pray together in their churches during the Covid pandemic, so they prayed in the fields, as their ancestors had prayed during times of persecution.

5

Leper Colonies

With the lockdown in full force, the cardinal-archbishop of one of America's largest archdioceses is celebrating Mass. There is no congregation in the cathedral, of course; the liturgy is being livestreamed. The viewer can see that there is no one near the cardinal; a single deacon stands at a decorous distance. Still the cardinal is wearing a mask—not on his face, actually, but suspended under his chin.

When the time comes for Communion, the cardinal ostentatiously rubs his hands with sanitizer. Then, as if that were not enough, he dons a full plastic face shield, of the type worn by dentists or surgeons. Thus girded against infection, he administers Communion—to just one person, the deacon—before returning to the altar to finish the liturgy.

Having accepted the argument that churches should be shut down in the spring to curb the spread of the Covid virus, American bishops were at pains to show, when they cautiously reopened their churches, that they were taking every precaution against infection. In one diocese after another the chancery churned out directives, informing pastors of the "best practices" that must be adopted when the faithful were allowed once more inside the churches.

The congregations must be small: no more than one hundred people, or fifty, or twenty, or even ten — according to the local government regulations. All members of the congregation must wear masks, and in a few cases, gloves as well. The faithful must maintain a "social distance" of six feet (considerably more than the World Health Organization standard of one meter). Pews must be sanitized after every Mass. Alternate pews must be roped off. Arrows must be taped to the floor to indicate the one-way flow of traffic in the aisles.

There were new liturgical directives, too. The priest-celebrant was to wear a mask while distributing Communion; he and any other eucharistic ministers must sanitize their hands carefully. Processions and choral music were eliminated. If two or more priests concelebrated, each must use his own chalice. One bishop wrote a sixty-three-page document, detailing the steps that must be taken to maintain community safety standards. (How many bishops had ever given their priests such detailed instruction on how the liturgy should be conducted in order to maintain proper reverence for the Eucharist?)

The jittery fixation of church bureaucrats on the danger of infection was perhaps best illustrated in July when a lay worker at a parish in the Pittsburgh diocese tested positive for the Covid virus. The diocese quickly announced that the parish would be closed, cleaned, and sanitized. Not only that, but four other neighboring parishes would be closed as well, just as a precautionary measure!

The Few Plead for Access

As a general rule, the Catholics most anxious to implement tough Covid restrictions were those aligned with the liberal wing of the Church. On paper, that correlation might seem odd. Elderly

Catholics, generally acknowledged to be more conservative in their beliefs, were also more vulnerable to the disease. Younger people, restless and energetic, might be expected to chafe under restrictions. Yet it was the more orthodox Catholics who pleaded for greater access to the sacraments because these were the Catholics in whose eyes the sacramental life of the Church was most precious.

Surveys have consistently shown that only a minority of self-identified Catholics believe that Jesus Christ is truly present in the Eucharist. For that minority, participation in the Eucharistic liturgy is, understandably, a top priority. For those who see the Eucharist as symbolic and the Mass as a communal gathering, the liturgy is not so essential. In fact, a minority of American Catholics attend Sunday Mass regularly even in the best of circumstances; it should not be surprising that a large number, given the green light to skip Mass, found the leisure of Sunday mornings attractive.

Similarly, most Catholics only rarely make use of confession (or as it is formally known, the Sacrament of Reconciliation). It made very little difference in their lives if confessions were not being heard on a regular basis. But for devout Catholics who made a habit of frequent confession, this too was a disaster.

The remarkable deference that Church leaders showed to civil authority during the epidemic followed a pattern that has become all too common in the American Catholic community in recent years. For several decades, Church leaders have carefully avoided public confrontations with influential politicians, even at the expense of ecclesiastical discipline. This pattern has been most evident in the manifest unwillingness of American bishops to deny Communion to politicians who promote legal abortion.

For forty years, restive pro-life Catholics had been instructed that blatant disregard for human life—as demonstrated by a Catholic politician's endorsement of abortion on demand—is not sufficient reason to deny anyone the Eucharist. Yet now, in a sudden reversal, Church leaders said that the cause of life—the need to protect innocent people from a dangerous virus—was sufficient reason to deny the Eucharist to *everyone*.

We could not keep our churches open, we were told, because the Catholic Church is a pro-life institution, and we must never do anything that would jeopardize the lives of those who come to worship with us. A cynic might wonder whether that argument had been crafted precisely to silence the devout pro-life Catholics who were most frustrated with the restrictions on the sacraments. But the logic of the argument has a strong, albeit superficial, appeal. What it misses is the crucial distinction between a willful attack on the life of an innocent human being and a death from disease, which no one willed.

The fundamental problem with the "pro-life" argument was that it did not go far enough. The Catholic Church is not in the business of saving lives but the business of saving souls. Or rather, the Church is dedicated to saving *eternal* lives. During an epidemic, while civil leaders rightly have the physical health of their people uppermost on their minds, Church leaders ought to be more mindful of the spiritual welfare of their flocks. As important as it may be to worry about the physical health of parishioners—and few people were disputing the need for caution—pastors should never do anything to jeopardize souls.

Only rarely do the demands of physical health come into conflict with the demands of spiritual welfare. But such a conflict arose in this case. Different pastors resolved the conflict in different ways, trying their best to strike a balance between the competing claims. But far too many pastors, rather than making their own decisions, deferred entirely to worldly priorities.

From Bad Taste to Sacrilege

In March, during the first days of the lockdown, when Americans were told to live under restrictions for a few weeks to "flatten the curve," the quick acceptance of government mandates was understandable. Americans were frightened by the prospect of a deadly pandemic and ready to take extraordinary precautions. But as the weeks rolled on and we gained a more accurate perspective on the dangers of the virus, the restrictions appeared far less reasonable.

Eventually states began—ever so slowly, gradually, cautiously—to allow the churches to reopen. But government mandates still restricted the size of congregations, and in defiance of any scientific logic, the number of people allowed into a cavernous Catholic cathedral was no greater than the number allowed in a tiny Protestant meetinghouse.

Meanwhile, the abject fear of Covid infection had led some pastors to make their own changes to the liturgy: changes that in some cases were absurd, tasteless, or downright sacrilegious. Thus, in one church the pastor baptized children by shooting water at them from a squirt gun, while wearing a mask, face shield, and rubber gloves to protect himself from the grave danger posed by an infant. In another, an "at home" First Communion service was arranged, in which parents were given consecrated hosts, to be administered to their children at the appropriate time during a livestreamed Mass. In yet another, the pastor consecrated hosts and packed them into small envelopes, to be picked up by parishioners as they left the church. The parishioners would then each take an envelope—having first dropped their own envelopes into a collection basket—and take it outside, having been instructed to leave immediately.

In many churches, parishioners were turned away at the door if they had not signed up to reserve a place in the pews. Some parishes built Plexiglass cages, like those found in banks, so that the Eucharist could be dispensed through a slot, with no contact between the minister and the communicant, both of whom were masked. Some required bride and groom to stand six feet apart, wearing masks, throughout a wedding ceremony—in slavish obedience to civil rules, without any thought to the complete self-giving and unity the marriage vows promise.

One liturgical supply company set a high standard for tastelessness, offering for sale a metal dispenser—like the odd coin dispensers carried by bus drivers in years past—in which priests could pack the consecrated hosts and drop them into the hands of parishioners. To the best of my knowledge, no Catholic priest actually used this hideous device. I hope that is the case. The image of a priest *dropping* the Body of Christ out of a metal container is too horrendous for the Catholic mind to contemplate.

But if the worst didn't happen, what did happen was bad enough. Public health authorities dictated the ways in which Catholic rites could be performed, and all too many clerics accepted the secular orders. A bishop (soon to be promoted to become the archbishop of a major see), accepting hospital rules that barred chaplains from entering the rooms of Covid patients, authorized the ministers to delegate their authority and let nurses anoint the sick. That policy was vetoed by the Vatican, since it ignored both the essential power of the priest to administer the last rites and the insistence of the Church that the sacraments must be conveyed in person. For similar reasons, the Vatican ruled against a proposal to allow confessions by telephone.

Since priests and even bishops were willing to experiment with even the essential elements of the sacraments, one could hardly blame secular public health officials for doing the same. An earnest priest, turned away from a nursing home when he sought to bring the Eucharist to elderly residents, received a helpful reply from an equally earnest resident who was willing to "look into purchasing pre-packed communion sets" if that would be acceptable. Who could blame her, when some parishes were doing exactly what she proposed?

One enterprising priest at a major American archdiocese recruited a group of fellow priests who were willing to go into hospitals, accepting the risks, to bring the sacraments to the sick and dying. Unfortunately, their offer was rejected by the hospitals — although the institutions helpfully suggested that they might speak to patients over the phone. The frustrated priest who had spearheaded the effort looked to the archdiocese for guidance and reported that "the cardinal commented that the important thing is that we offered." Yes, the archdiocese had earned a bit of good will with the hospitals by making the offer — and then by accepting the rejection. But the patients still did not receive the sacraments, and *that* was "the important thing."

Tougher Than the Rules

Many Catholic pastors, anxious to satisfy both the demands of public health authorities and the worries of nervous parishioners, instituted their own special restrictions, tougher than the local mandates. One Canadian bishop boasted that his rules for parish activities "go beyond the requirements in most health unit orders and local bylaws." He required that everyone wear a mask in church, or — if they suffered from a medical condition that prevented wearing a mask — present a signed letter from a medical professional attesting to the condition. Those recalcitrant parishioners who refused to wear masks, the bishop said, should be notified by registered mail "that they will not be allowed into the church should they present themselves again."

Another bishop ruled that masks must be worn by any parishioner over the age of two. He apparently understood that it was unreasonable to expect a younger toddler to wear a mask, but he proposed a stunning solution: any family with children under the age of two should stay away! Thus, the youngest children—the Catholics of the future—would be barred from their own parishes and their parents made to understand that, unless they left their children at home, they were unwelcome as well. ("The disciples rebuked the people; but Jesus said, 'Let the children come to me, and do not hinder them; for to such belongs the kingdom of heaven'" [Matt. 19:13–14].)

Far more common was the practice of requiring parishioners to register in advance for a place at Mass. Having taken down names and addresses, the parishes could then cooperate with public officials in "contact tracing," enabling authorities to order a quarantine for anyone who was in the same building with someone who tested positive for the Covid virus. The same contact-tracing regimen was also in effect in many parishes for confessions—in clear violation of the principle that every Catholic has the right to confess without revealing his identity.

How could pastors justify these violations of established Catholic norms? Some bishops insisted that their people should look on the bright side of the restrictions, and one Irish prelate wrote that the lockdown "has enabled us to spend quality time with family members in the home, providing opportunities for understanding, encouragement, affirmation, and development." But of course, the lockdown did not *enable* anyone to spend quality time at home; that opportunity had always been available. The lockdown *forced* people to stay at home. And while for some families the extra time together produced the benefits that the archbishop cited, in other homes it led to conflicts, resentments, and even violence.

Stay Away to Stay Together

An American archbishop suggested that by shutting down parishes, the Church was imitating Jesus Christ, who healed the sick: "The closure of inside Mass is itself a type of 'preemptive healing' by helping people avoid acquiring a potentially deadly disease." So now priests were encouraged to think of themselves as miracle-workers whenever they turned the key on the parish church door.

Writing for *Catholic World Report*, Douglas Farrow remarked that many Catholics — not just clerics — were captivated by the logic of "healing" their neighbors:

> They make their appeal to the fifth commandment, "Thou shalt not kill." And to what Jesus identified as the second Great Commandment, "Love thy neighbor as thyself." These they have merged into a justification for the new Covid commandment: "Thou shalt love thy neighbor by staying well away from him, lest thou pass on a virus that might kill him."

While readily conceding the need for prudence in attending to health concerns, Farrow added that a sense of balance and proportion is necessary because "it won't do to protect people from a deadly virus only to hand them over to poverty, famine, tyranny, war, or death by neglect." Yet even that was not his primary concern. The greater danger, Farrow argued, lay in the willingness of Church officials to accept government-imposed restrictions — even extreme restrictions — without demanding that the government understand the Church's priorities.

> My worry is that by their compliance they are endorsing, or will be seen to be endorsing, not the gospel of the kingdom but the gospel of the state; that they are making the priorities of the state their own, rather than the priorities of Jesus.

When Catholics in the United Kingdom made a plea for access to the sacraments, a spokesman for the Bishops' Conference of England and Wales expressed sympathy for their "understandable" desires. But he patiently explained that "there are other factors that need to be considered," including "a moral duty to protect life" and to "heed the best professional advice about the dangers of this virus."

Here the laudable desire to preserve public health clashed directly with the natural instinct (and it is more than an instinct) to worship God as a community. By allowing the former to override the latter, the bishops were ignoring the sort of wisdom that Pope Pius XII expressed in *Mediator Dei* in 1947, when he said:

> Every impulse of the human heart, besides, expresses itself naturally through the senses; and the worship of God, being the concern not merely of individuals but of the whole community of mankind, must therefore be social as well.... Exterior worship, finally, reveals and emphasizes the unity of the mystical Body, feeds new fuel to its holy zeal, fortifies its energy, intensifies its action day by day.

Livestream Masses, private prayer at home, and pious pleas about preserving health could not substitute for the outward communal

worship that is the life of the Catholic Church. In a provoca-
tive column published in July, after three months of restricted
parish activity, Msgr. Charles Pope lamented that the Church
had "cowered and capitulated" in a time of crisis. "We have not
summoned people to trust and faith," he wrote with regret.

"Isn't there more to living than just not dying or not getting
sick?" Msgr. Pope continued. "Will we simply reflect the beliefs
and opinions of the current culture, or will we influence it with
a theology that insists that suffering and death have meaning
and an important role in our lives?"

In an article that appeared on the same day, in the French
journal *Le Figaro*, Cardinal Robert Sarah, the prefect of the Vatican's Congregation for Divine Worship, made a similar point,
expressing concerns that Church leaders, in their desire to be
"good citizens," had too often lost sight of their more important
mission. Yes, the Church works for the good of society at large and
offers her guidance on temporal affairs, as befits (in the words of
Pope Paul VI), an "expert on humanity." However, the cardinal
wrote, "little by little Christians have come to forget the reason
for that expertise."

Who Guides Whom?

The Catholic Church can offer advice to civic leaders, in pursuit
of the common good, because the Church knows what mankind needs in order to find true and lasting happiness. But civic
leaders cannot return the favor; they cannot offer the same sort
of guidance to the Church because the secular world does not
comprehend the Church's mission of salvation. The Church un-
derstands the world; the world does not understand the Church.

So the Church cannot, indeed must not, accept the presumption that the state knows what is good for the Church or for

the faithful. The state's business is to know what is good for the temporal welfare of citizens in general. When the state's laws are designed for that purpose and equitably enforced, the Church does well to obey them. But when the state arbitrarily rules that church services are not essential activities, the Church cannot acquiesce. Worship is essential. The Church knows that because she is an "expert on humanity" and because she is familiar with the First Commandment. To accept the designation as "nonessential" is to deny the proper authority of Christ's Church.

When civil officials issue orders about what is good for public health, Catholic bishops should listen because civil officials have the proper authority to enforce public health rules. Indeed, a prudent bishop would ordinarily heed those rules *even if he personally believed they were misguided*, because the bishop is not an expert in the field of public health. But if and when the rules infringe on the prerogatives of the Church — if they compromise the evangelical mission — then the bishop must demur, and protest, and if necessary, defy the civil authority. And so must lay Catholics.

Ironically, within a few weeks after the appearance of his column urging the faithful not to fear the Covid virus, Msgr. Pope himself contracted the disease and spent a few days under hospital care before making his recovery. Some Catholics, who resented his criticism of the lockdown, seemed to take his illness as a sign that his entire attitude was wrong; one prominent Catholic commentator lashed out with more than twenty inflammatory Twitter messages in the space of a single day, charging that the priest had been insensitive and irresponsible.

Actually, Msgr. Pope had anticipated that reaction, even before he fell ill. "No doubt some readers will think me imprudent, irresponsible, and insensitive," he wrote in his original column.

He had never denied the severity of the epidemic, nor had he recommended against reasonable safeguards. He had simply insisted that the Church could not "remain fearfully silent," and the sacramental life of the Church must continue even under duress.

Emerging from the hospital, Msgr. Pope made it clear that his views had not been changed by his own physical struggle. He wrote a new column, affirming that "my concern remains that our fears are out of proportion to the actual risks." The fundamental lesson to be learned, he stressed, was that "in a secular world where suffering and death have lost all meaning, we must not succumb to meaninglessness."

A Disappointing Vatican Statement

Unfortunately, no such clarion call to evangelization could be heard from Rome. In July, the Pontifical Academy for Life, under the leadership of the controversial Archbishop Vincenzo Paglia, released a dense document on the epidemic. The Vatican press office introduced it with a title as prolix as the document itself: "Useful Information on the Document of the Pontifical Academy for Life: *Humana Communitas* in the Age of Pandemic: Untimely Meditations on Life's Rebirth." That title was misleading; the document provided very little useful information. But it was, indeed, "untimely." There is never a good time for this sort of vapid rumination.

Even in describing the unhappy social situation arising from the pandemic, the Pontifical Academy was mawkishly sentimental (not to mention excessively wordy):

> It has deprived us of the exuberance of embraces, the kindness of hand shakings, the affection of kisses, and turned relations into fearful interactions among strangers,

the neutral exchange of faceless individualities shrouded
in the anonymity of protective gears.

Opening with a sketch of the damage that the pandemic has
done to human community, the document observes: "Surely,
we are summoned to the courage of resistance." But nowhere
did the Pontifical Academy guide us toward the source of such
courageous resistance. Despite stretching to well over four thousand words, the Vatican document did not mention God, Jesus
Christ, the Holy Spirit, the Church, the sacraments, prayer, or
even charity; even the word "Christian" did not appear in the
text. There was admittedly a call for "moral conversion," but
in context it was clearly a call for an ideological rather than
religious conversion.

The Pontifical Academy for Life, you see, regarded the pandemic as a condign punishment for mankind's sins against the
environment: "The Covid-19 epidemic has much to do with our
depredation of the earth and the despoiling of its intrinsic value."
Obviously, that is not a scientific statement. But it might be taken
as a religious claim if the religion in question is environmentalism.

From the Vatican, however, one expects a Christian message:
a message of hope that is sadly lacking in this statement. Under
different leadership, in a different era, the Pontifical Academy
for Life might have urged us not to be paralyzed by fear of sick-
ness and death, nor to regard any interaction with neighbors as a
dangerous imposition. The document made a weak gesture in that
direction, saying that "the seeds of hope have been sown in the
obscurity of small gestures, in acts of solidarity too many to count,
too precious to broadcast." But it did not catalogue the "small
gestures" that Christians might make; instead, it made a grandi-
ose call for worldwide solidarity and international cooperation,

stipulating that the World Health Organization should have a "privileged place" in the campaign.

The pandemic had struck fear—often irrational fear—into millions of hearts. The Vatican *should* have been offering reassurance and perspective, reminding the world that death is not the greatest tragedy; that life has meaning; and that, armed with the gifts of the Holy Spirit, we could conquer our fears. This Christian perspective is sadly lacking from this document.

"The lessons of fragility, finitude, and vulnerability bring us to the threshold of a new vision," the Pontifical Academy instructed us. Yes, but only to the threshold, and this document failed to usher us across—failed even to invite us into the life of Christ.

Into the Common Good

In justifying restrictions on the sacraments, Church leaders routinely fell into a familiar trap: defining the common good as it was perceived by secular leaders. Preserving public health is undoubtedly an important aspect of the common good. But by invoking the common good, Church leaders too often were implicitly accepting the vision of public welfare presented by politicians who might, on other issues, be thoroughly hostile to Catholic social teachings. How could Catholic bishops and priests accept the perception of the common good advanced by political leaders who supported legal abortion on demand or same-sex marriage? How could they accept a notion of the common good that did not preserve the right and duty of the people to engage in public worship?

To be candid, Catholic bishops in the United States were in a weak position to criticize public figures, having absorbed heavy fire for two decades because of their mishandling of the sex-abuse scandal. No doubt bishops were fearful that in any public confrontation with secular authorities, they would lose still more public sympathy. Those fears were aggravated by the knowledge that within the Church, even among the most devout of the faithful, there were many so nervous about the epidemic that they were ready to support the most draconian restrictions.

So now perhaps bishops were overly anxious to show that they could act as good citizens—that they would obey the laws (which they had not done in sex-abuse cases). They were determined to act as responsible leaders in society, bringing the people together in support of the commonly shared goal of public health. No doubt they were also motivated by a genuine desire to prevent churches from becoming sites for "superspreader" infections, as well as perhaps a less noble desire to avoid negative publicity, lawsuits, and public clashes with secular authorities.

However—as so often happens, sadly, when Church leaders set their pastoral sights by secular standards—the effort was counterproductive. Church officials explained that they had accepted restrictions on worship in defense of the dignity of human life. They wanted—so badly!—to preserve their communities. But the lockdown was destroying those communities.

Austin Ruse made the point in an August column for *Crisis*, with a headline that told the story: "Covid Has Made All of Us Lepers." In the time of Christ, lepers were forced to live outside the community, as pariahs. Now masks and "social distancing" were forcing *everyone* to live in isolation, treating others as potential threats, avoiding human contact. *"Can we ever walk this back?"* Ruse wondered. "Can our fellow man ever become our fellow man again?"

The Saints' Examples

And what if the worst of our fears were realized, and the epidemic spread at a much faster rate—and with deadlier effect—so that every one of our neighbors really *did* pose a threat to our own health? How should Christians react to that sort of pandemic? St. Damien of Molokai, who plunged into the leper community in order to serve the outcasts, offers the model of true Christian service. Yes, he did eventually become a leper himself; he sacrificed his life in service, in imitation of Christ. That sacrifice is perfectly rational from a Christian perspective, and the Church honors Damien the Leper as a saint.

Needless to say, a society that sees death as the ultimate defeat cannot understand, nor even accept, the choice that St. Damien made. But again, every Christian should understand, and the Church should constantly reaffirm that understanding, by both teaching and public practice.

Another model of Christian zeal, St. Peter Faber, the companion of St. Ignatius, founder of the Jesuit order, reported that in working with the sick he realized "that a person engaged in that kind of service or in any other kind of good work solely for the sake of Christ should be ready to lay down his life gladly at that work in whatever place he may find himself."

These saints could make extraordinary sacrifices, in part because they were celibate religious, without direct responsibilities for the care of their spouses and children. Lay Catholics, living in families, have more complicated choices to make about the dangers of infection. Yet bear in mind that these saints worked with people who *were* sick and *did* pose the threat of infection. The Covid epidemic presented a far less immediate threat.

Within a parish church, if only a tiny percentage of people could contract the virus from a chance and fleeting encounter with someone who was already infected, and if only a tiny percentage of the people so gathered could be presumed to carry the Covid virus, and if 99 percent of those who did contract the virus would survive the disease — in most cases, without experiencing serious symptoms — then the need for caution weighs much less heavily in the balance against the need for the sacraments. When a healthy productive citizen stays home, there is a cost to society. And when a healthy Christian stays away from church, there is a cost to the People of God.

6

Taking Sacraments Seriously

Imagine a primitive tribe somewhere, whose shamans perform a ritual rain dance each year. Now imagine that the region where the tribe lives is struck by a terrible drought. The drought is so bad that the people are thirsty, so bad that whenever they walk, they raise clouds of dust.

Now imagine that the time has come for the annual rain dance. But the elders of the tribe tell the shamans that this year they must not dance. The effort would increase their thirst, raising clouds of dust, making everyone else thirsty, at a time when that thirst could not be satisfied.

If the elders made that ruling, would you think that the tribe really believed in the efficacy of the rain dance?

Christians do not perform rain dances, nor do we believe that God will provide rain on command whenever we pray for it. (Although He might; ask Elijah.) But we do believe in the efficacy of prayer. Don't we?

In times of great need, it should be an instinctive reaction for Christians to turn to God in prayer. During the Covid epidemic most of us have felt a great need—not only for healing and for safety and for a cure, but also for peace of mind, for a restoration of what we have lost, and perhaps, above all, for hope. In the course of 2020, we Americans have frequently been asked to pray for those who are sick or dying. But rarely have Christians demanded the lead role in our society's response to this health crisis. Shouldn't we have been telling civic leaders, when they suggested restricting public worship: "Look, you *need* our prayers; you *need* our public celebration of the Mass. This is your best chance for relief from the scourge!"

The Mass was and is our best hope for two reasons. First, because the Mass is the perfect form of worship to almighty God, the God who controls all life and all events on this earth. If God chooses to eliminate the Covid virus, or to make us all immune, or to give someone the inspiration to discover a cure, He can do so. Our prayers at Mass are the best way to plead for that relief. But even if He chooses not to make that sort of extraordinary intervention in human affairs, our prayers raise our own sights, putting the current danger in perspective, protecting us against the sort of precipitous panic that threatens society at least as much as the virus itself.

The keepers of fashionable public opinion have encouraged us obsessively to put our trust in flimsy face masks, our hope in the pharmaceutical companies working to produce vaccines. What might happen if we put the same communal energies into prayer? We don't know because communal prayer has been discouraged — even by many religious leaders.

Of course we can pray by ourselves, in the privacy of our own homes. But Christians have been taught by the Lord Himself that there is special power in common prayer: "where two or three are gathered in my name." A coincidental meeting of two or three people would be acceptable even under the most draconian lockdown rules. But any *gathering* is viewed with suspicion. In some cities the rules have allowed only one person at a time to pray privately inside a church: even a cathedral that could hold several thousand. And most pastors have meekly accepted those rules.

Fasting

In times of trouble, the practice traditionally taught to loyal Catholics was to redouble the intensity of their prayer. This year, however, the directives that American Catholics received from their shepherds often pointed in the opposite direction. The lockdowns began during Lent: a season of prayer and fasting. Strange, then, that several bishops told their people that they would be dispensed from the traditional ban on eating meat during Fridays in Lent.

One bishop explained that he was lifting that ban in light of "many other sacrifices that we are suddenly experiencing." He was evidently assuming that everyone had the same experiences that he had and reacted the same way. Even so he was failing to explain the traditional Catholic practice of "offering up" one's sufferings, uniting them to the sacrifice of Christ. He further missed the mark insofar as a *voluntary* sacrifice, like giving up meat, has far more spiritual value than the suffering one cannot avoid. Indeed suffering, in itself, is not a sacrifice; it only takes on a spiritual dimension when it is willingly endured. When we are battered by events that we cannot control, that is the time when it is *most* important to intensify our spiritual discipline, so that we will have the resources we need to meet extraordinary challenges.

Look at the question in a different way. In Catholic practice, prayer and fasting are inextricably linked, particularly during Lent. (Actually, there are three elements to the traditional Lenten routine: prayer, fasting, and almsgiving. We can be quite certain that no bishop suggested that Catholics should be *less* generous with their contributions to the parish or their diocese during a time of epidemic.) It is difficult to imagine a Catholic bishop encouraging his people to ease up on their prayer during Lent. So why should healthy Catholics, who are not in special need of the calories, ease up on their fasting? We were all facing special challenges during the Lent of 2020, but I did not find in the Gospel any advice from the Lord that "this kind is cast out only by cheeseburgers."

Last Rites

Lenten fasting and penance are practices tied to a recognition that we are all sinners in need of redemption. That same recognition of our sinful nature is addressed, in the regular life of the Church, by sacramental confession and the last rites. Confession, alas, became difficult to manage during the lockdown, when churches were closed, and priests were ordered to stay away from their people. Even the last rites were curtailed. Since the Second Vatican Council, Catholics had been encouraged to make use of the anointing—not just when they were nearing death but when they were in some danger of death or simply in need of healing. Now suddenly that advice was reversed; the faithful were instructed that they could not expect the comfort of the sacrament unless they were in extremis—and even then, they could not be sure that a priest would come to them.

A friend of mine, a priest who served as a chaplain in Iraq, was decorated for heroism when, during a heated battle, he rushed to the side of a man who had been mortally wounded in order to give him a final blessing. The dying man was lying helpless on the ground where, obviously, the enemy had trained their sights on him. My friend could now have been in the same crosshairs; he revealed later that he expected to die. He administered the sacrament, nevertheless, because that was his mission: to serve as a priest, *in persona Christi,* to give his life to save others. His ministry was more important to him than his life.

When a crisis strikes, we reveal what is important to us, as individuals and as a society. We as a society clearly do not believe in the power of prayer; we don't consider religion essential. The churches were closed before the bars and restaurants were shut down. Surely the virus was more likely to spread in places where people sat elbow-to-elbow, eating and drinking, than when they were seated quietly in pews. But public officials were reluctant to impose what would inevitably be unpopular orders.

Priorities

People must eat, the authorities reasoned. At first, restaurants continued to serve meals. People need exercise, so gyms were not immediately shut down. People need to go to work, so subways and buses continued to run, bringing people into close proximity with strangers. Mothers need to work, so, still more remarkably, day-care centers remained open and even in some cases expanded their services. (Children were generally immune from the Covid infection, we were reassured. But the teachers and parents who gathered daily at these centers were not.)

Yes, people do need to eat; but with rare exceptions, they could prepare and eat their food at home. Yes, people should exercise; and the great outdoors beckons, with parks and hiking trails and bike paths that preserve social distance. And yes, people need to work, but at what cost did society preserve some employment options, after having closed down others? Thus we revealed our priorities. Our political leaders judged—rightly, for the most part—that Americans would not tolerate the abrupt closure of restaurants, bars, gyms, and day-care centers; but they would tolerate the closing of churches.

Personally, I was not terribly surprised that politicians made that judgment, nor that the vast majority of Americans accepted it. But I was astounded by the cavalier attitude displayed by Catholic leaders about the restrictions on sacramental ministry. The very first pastoral priority of a Catholic bishop is, or should be, to ensure that the faithful have access to the sacraments. Yet within a few weeks after the lockdowns began in March 2020, the public celebration of Mass ended in most of the dioceses of the United States. Baptisms and weddings and funerals were restricted, deferred, or cancelled outright. Priests were not available to hear confessions. This was an unprecedented disaster: a suffering that American Catholics had never experienced or even contemplated.

When they made their decisions to suspend the public celebration of the Mass, many bishops issued statements couched in the language of bureaucrats rather than pastors. They did not give the faithful the very necessary reassurance that at least the daily celebration of the eucharistic sacrifice would continue, albeit behind closed doors. They did not convey an understanding of how the faithful would suffer, much less express sympathy for that suffering.

How could it possibly have been right that when pastors were instructed to stop celebrating Mass for their people, the directive came not directly from their bishop but from a public relations consultant? How could it be right that at a time when political leaders were saying that the shutdown would last for a couple of weeks, the bishops in one American state had already announced that there would be no public celebrations for Easter, without waiting to see how the next few weeks might change the situation?

Worship in a Time of Real Persecution

During the years when the Soviet empire persecuted the Church, a pastor who had worked with refugees and dissidents told a story about Christians in a *gulag* camp, who had petitioned their jailers for permission to celebrate Easter with a prayer service. The pitiless commandant replied that they could hold their service — in a pond on the grounds of the prison camp, where the water had not yet fully thawed. He thought this cruel "concession" would be enough to crush the unwelcome manifestation of religious faith. He was wrong. On Easter Sunday morning, the stalwart Christian inmates waded into the icy water to pray together. For them, worship was the top priority. For most American Catholics, though, Easter 2020 passed quietly — without a communal prayer service, let alone a public Mass.

For Catholics who truly believe what they profess, the Mass should be the top priority. How much should a believer be willing to sacrifice, to be present at the Sacrifice of Calvary? How much risk should he tolerate, to consume the Body and Blood of Christ? In the sixth chapter of St. John's Gospel, Jesus gives a very clear indication of why the Eucharist should be paramount:

> Truly, truly, I say to you, unless you eat the flesh of the Son of Man and drink his blood, you have no life in you; he who eats my flesh and drinks my blood has eternal life.

For anyone who believes those words, it is perfectly rational to risk one's life in order to attend Mass and receive Communion. After all, without it we have no life; with it we have the promise that we will never die. Many thousands of Catholics, clinging to their faith through times of persecution, have risked their lives to attend Mass. Could we not risk the remote chance of infection with a disease—from which the vast majority of sufferers would recover quickly?

In 2011, not quite a decade before the Covid crisis, Cardinal Sean O'Malley of Boston issued a pastoral letter on the importance of Sunday Mass, in which he recalled the heroism of the Christians under persecution during the reign of the Roman Emperor Diocletian. When forbidden to celebrate the Sabbath, they replied, "*Sine dominico non possumus*"—"Without Sunday we cannot live." Cardinal O'Malley wrote:

> In fact, for nearly 2,000 years Christians have risked their lives to participate in Sunday Mass. During the Reformation in England, priests were martyred when caught offering Holy Mass for English Catholics. Courageous lay people who gave their homes over as places of Catholic worship, and who harbored priests, suffered torture and death.

Going on to praise the many thousands of Catholics who willingly suffered to attend Mass under persecution in the twentieth century, the cardinal wrote: "We give thanks to God that we do not have to put our lives in jeopardy to attend Mass at our local parish." Just a few years later, the same Cardinal O'Malley would tell the Catholics of Boston that they were not required to attend Sunday Mass. But more than that: they *could not* imitate the Catholic martyrs that he had held up as models because he had forbidden the public celebration of the Mass.

Catholics who were horrified by the cancellation of public Masses found little sympathy from their pastors. Bishops and priests accused them of being uncharitable when they pleaded for the opening of the churches. They would not only be risking their lives by coming to Mass, the pastors told them; they would be irresponsibly risking the lives of others. A desire to participate in the eucharistic sacrifice, the source and summit of Catholic spiritual life, was taken as evidence of an unchristian attitude.

Rules are rules, we were reminded. The bishop sets the rules for liturgical worship within his diocese, and his decisions should not be challenged. But what if his decisions are based not on his pastoral judgment but on his understanding of public health questions? Catholics believe that a bishop can call upon the grace proper to his authority when he addresses pastoral issues, but on questions of public health he has no more or less authority than the members of his flock.

Conditioning the Sacraments

When the public celebration of Mass was partially restored (at least in some places), bishops painstakingly set forth precise safety rules, dictating the wearing of face masks, the proper distance between seats, the procedures for sanitizing hands and pews and liturgical vessels. Were these pastoral decisions, designed to ensure proper reverence? Certainly not; they were public health guidelines. And whether or not they made sense in terms of safeguarding public health (a question that was and is open to dispute), they frequently had a deleterious effect on the sense of reverence, the understanding of the liturgy, and the belief in the Real Presence.

Take, for example, the use of sanitizer. A bottle of commercial sanitizer became a prominent feature in the sanctuary. The priest scrubbed his hands when he approached the altar, then scrubbed them again before distributing Communion. Now what had happened, between the Offertory and Communion, that require a new round of sanitizing? Having confected the Eucharist, the priest now turned away from the consecrated host — from the Body of Christ — to address himself to the sanitizer. The most conspicuous rituals of the liturgy revolved around that bottle of sanitizer. The aroma of sanitizer filled the air, as incense had filled it in happier times.

Then, having finished his ablutions, the priest donned a mask before distributing Communion to the people. The mask itself was a counter-witness for the priest, who stood in the place of Christ. "Hide not thy face from me," the psalmist prayed to God. The faithful came forward, themselves masked, carefully staying several feet away from each other, treating other members of the community as potential threats. Then they were encouraged to leave the church quickly, without pausing to speak to each other. In some parishes they received Communion as they filed out of the church and were instructed to consume the Eucharist in the parking lot. And this was the "communal meal"—the aspect of the liturgy that was, prior to the Covid era, so much emphasized by liberal Catholics? This was the sacrament of Christian unity?

But Catholics who objected to the deliberate uglification of the eucharistic liturgy found little sympathy in diocesan chanceries. The bishops knew what was best; yet again they showed little patience with those impractical pious Catholics who longed for more reverent worship.

If You Don't Like It, Stay Home

In May, the editorial board of *Our Sunday Visitor*, a weekly firmly anchored in the mainstream of American Catholicism, rebuked Catholics who protested the new liturgical rules. If the faithful did not like the restricted liturgy, the editors suggested that they should stay home:

> If you'd prefer not to wear a mask to Mass, for example, you could watch or listen to the liturgy from your car and

ask your pastor if he will accommodate a private reception of Communion afterward. Alternatively, if you believe it is too early for parishes to resume public worship and are uncomfortable attending, you could simply stay home and continue the spiritual practices you have developed in recent weeks.

In Tennessee, Bishop Rick Stika of Knoxville was not nearly so gentle with his critics. After battling with parishioners who resisted the mandatory wearing of masks, he declared in December that he would simply bar the dissidents from the church:

> No one will be admitted to any of our churches without a mask. If they insist, Mass will not start until all have on a mask and keep a social distance. If the mask is taken off, I have instructed our priests to stop the celebration of Mass until the masks are worn.

Here again the bishop's ukase undermined a proper understanding of the Mass, not to mention a strange insistence on the redundant measures of both masking and distancing. If the liturgy were merely a community observance, temporarily wrapped up in emergency public health protocols, then maybe such a stern legalistic approach could be warranted. But if a priest truly understood that he was engaged in the Sacrifice of Calvary, how could he possibly stop to reprimand a parishioner? Let us hope that at least some priests in Knoxville were too thoroughly absorbed in the eucharistic drama, too occupied with the most important work they could do, to be distracted by such trivia.

With their rigid insistence on masks, our bishops betrayed a newfound interest in what the faithful were wearing to Mass. They had not been so vocal, so clear, and so persistent before the

Covid epidemic. They had not instructed their pastors to bar the church doors to parishioners who arrived in halter tops, cut-off denim shorts, or T-shirts bearing tasteless slogans. Ordinary decorum had not seemed so important; establishing an atmosphere of respect and reverence had not seemed so important. The mask mandate, too, showed that public health considerations had trumped concern for liturgical propriety.

Most American bishops, if they insisted on masks in church, allowed an exemption for people with medical conditions that made it difficult or impossible to wear a mask. No doubt some perfectly healthy people took advantage of that exemption. This created a challenge for pastors. Looking out over his congregation on a Sunday morning, seeing dozens of people unmasked, a priest would know that not everyone had a qualifying medical condition. But he would not know *which* parishioners were violating the bishop's orders.

Then again, priests have faced a similar challenge for generations. Poll after poll shows that the vast majority of Catholic married couples use contraceptives, in violation of Church teaching. Priests know that many of their parishioners are engaged in this gravely sinful behavior, but they cannot know which couples are guilty. I have never heard a priest at any ordinary parish say in a sermon that married Catholics who use contraceptives should not receive Communion. Yet in the past year I have heard several sermons in which priests said that those who do not wear masks should not enter the church.

"I find it outrageous," Bishop Stika wrote, "for some to use the idea of wearing a mask as some government control." In an odd sense he was right, at least insofar as his own directive was concerned. It was not the government that was imposing control on the faithful of Knoxville; it was the bishop.

A Tendency to Rebuke Piety

The degradation of the liturgy during the Covid epidemic was most painful to the most pious Catholics: to those who ache for a Mass that accentuates the transcendent. But to tell the truth, those Catholics have become accustomed, over the years, to rebukes from their bishops. In 1985, Dietrich von Hildebrand wrote in *The Devastated Vineyard* that

> it is most especially infuriating when certain bishops, who themselves show this lethargy toward heretics, assume a rigorously authoritarian attitude toward those believers who are fighting for orthodoxy, and who are thus doing what the bishops ought to be doing themselves.... They want to silence the faithful believers who take up the cause of orthodoxy, the very people who should, by all rights, be the joy of the bishops' hearts, their consolation, a source of strength for overcoming their own lethargy. Instead, these people are regarded as disturbers of the peace....
>
> For they [the bishops] have nothing to fear from the orthodox: the orthodox do not control the mass media or the press; they are not the representatives of public opinion. And because of their submission to ecclesiastical authority, the fighters for orthodoxy will never be as aggressive as the so-called progressives. If they are reprimanded or disciplined, their bishops run no risk of being attacked by the liberal press and being defamed as reactionary.

The frustration of orthodox Catholics is not a new phenomenon, then; it certainly did not begin with the Covid era. The epidemic, along with the bishops' reactions to the crisis, highlighted a problem that has been growing within the Catholic Church for decades. The marked decline of reverence in the liturgy, the willingness to conform to secular culture, the failures of episcopal leadership, the loss of interest in the transcendent: all these trends have been discussed widely for years. Orthodox Catholics have become far more vocal, far more willing to criticize Church leaders, in the years since von Hildebrand's book was published.

The epidemic threw a bright new spotlight on the problem. Many Church leaders (not to mention many members of the faithful) clearly succumbed to the error—it really should be recognized as a heresy—that physical health is more important than spiritual health.

"In listening to and collaborating with civil authorities and experts," bishops and episcopal conferences "were prompt to make difficult and painful decisions, even to the point of suspending the participation of the faithful in the celebration of the Eucharist for a long period," wrote Cardinal Robert Sarah, the prefect of the Vatican's Congregation for Divine Worship, in August. However, he continued, the suspension of the sacraments could not continue indefinitely.

> We cannot be without the banquet of the Eucharist, the table of the Lord to which we are invited as sons and daughters, brothers and sisters, to receive the Risen Christ himself, present in body, blood, soul and divinity in that Bread of Heaven which sustains us in the joys and labors of this earthly pilgrimage.

The cardinal explained that while streamed or televised Masses "have performed a great service ... at a time when there was no possibility of community celebration, no broadcast is comparable to personal communication or can replace it. On the contrary, these broadcasts alone risk distancing us from a personal and intimate encounter with the incarnate God who gave himself to us not in a virtual way," but in the Eucharist. "As soon as circumstances permit," Cardinal Sarah wrote, it is "necessary and urgent" to restore the normal life of the Church.

When would "circumstances permit" the restoration of normal sacramental life? After the initial panic that produced the lockdown, some wise bishops recognized that a balance could be struck between the demands of public health and the requirements of liturgical reverence. In Baker, Oregon, for instance, Bishop Liam Cary issued guidelines in August that built upon the growing awareness of how the Covid virus was transmitted. He pointed out during Mass — and particularly during the reception of Communion — the priest and parishioners never stay close to each other for the fifteen minutes that was required to contract the virus. A momentary interaction, he said, was recognized by all public health officials as an "acceptable risk."

Dwelling in detail on the question of masks, Bishop Cary wrote:

> But physical hygiene is not the only consideration. Masks at the liturgy create serious symbolic confusion as well. At mass the priest takes the place of Jesus. Covering the face of the celebrant goes directly against the oft-repeated scriptural cry of the heart to God: "Hide not your face from me. Show me your face." In view of his sacred role in the liturgy ... a masked priest "would be a detrimental counter-sign" of division and danger rather than of openness and peace.

Bishop Cary, like Bishop Stika, asked members of the flock to wear masks in churches. But unlike his colleague in Tennessee, the

Oregon bishop was not anxious to demand compliance. "Those who are reluctant ... we should treat with patience and kindness; no one should be turned away from church."

Obviously, Bishop Cary, like every other responsible pastor, had been wrestling with the question of how to protect his people from disease. But he had not allowed that concern to overpower his primary concern for the welfare of souls. He had been planning to restore the normal sacramental life of the Church—as much as possible, as quickly as possible.

During the lockdown, when churches were closed, pastors had plenty of extra time on their hands to plan for the reopening. When the lockdown was partially lifted, some pastors already had their plans in place, while others were somehow caught off guard. The difference between these two types of pastors was not just a matter of perspective; it was also a matter of priorities. The priests in the former group were busily planning to restore the sacraments, determined to do whatever they could to serve the faithful, focused first on the spiritual welfare of their people. Let us hope and pray that from that group of energetic pastors—and exclusively from that group—the bishops of the future will be drawn.

7

Surrender to Caesar

The First Amendment to the U.S. Constitution guarantees that the government will not interfere with the free exercise of religion. The doctrine of the Catholic Church teaches that regular Sunday worship is not an option but a solemn obligation. Therefore, when the government prohibits regular attendance at Mass, it is violating the free exercise of the Catholic faith. So how is it that months after the Covid lockdown began, Catholic prelates are still accepting the demands of political leaders to restrict attendance at Mass?

In Massachusetts, where I currently reside, article II of the state constitution reads:

> It is the right *as well as the duty* of all men in society, publicly, and at stated seasons to worship the Supreme Being, the great Creator and Preserver of the universe. And no subject shall be hurt, molested, or restrained, in his person, liberty, or estate, for worshipping God in the manner and season most agreeable to the dictates of his own conscience. (emphasis added)

Yet here in Massachusetts, for the past eight months, the governor has set limits on the number of people who can attend Mass.

Those rules, set down not in law but in emergency orders—for an emergency that has no end in sight—appear to violate both the state and federal constitutions. Yet Catholic pastors are obeying them.

Earlier in this book I asked the question: When should the Catholic Church bow to the demands of the state? My own answer was and is simple: never. As I explained, the state has rightful authority to protect public health, but that authority is not unlimited; it does not override the freedom of the Church to pursue her mission. Freedom of religion is not a concession from the government. On the contrary, it is an inherent human right, a requirement of human dignity, which no government has any authority to usurp.

In May of 2020, the U.S. Conference of Catholic Bishops sent out a packet of material to promote the annual observance of Religious Freedom Week, which would come in June. The material included background information on adoption, health care policy, immigration, and the plight of religious minorities in Asia and Africa. It said nothing about the American civic officials who had curtailed or even banned the public celebration of Mass; nothing about the government officials who were dictating the appropriate ways for priests to hear confessions, anoint the sick, or distribute Communion; nothing about the classification of religious services as "nonessential" in states where liquor stores and marijuana dispensaries were tagged as "essential."

Why were the American bishops so quick to accept government restrictions, so reluctant to challenge orders of questionable validity and legality? Was it because they were beholden to the government for the tens of millions of dollars in contracts to Catholic charitable agencies? Or because they were fearful of any public conflict—especially conflict in courtrooms—after the battering they had taken during the years of the sex-abuse scandal? Or because their political sympathies were aligned with the politicians who issued the orders?

Whatever their reasons, the American bishops left it to the Evangelical churches and Jewish synagogues—bodies without the same sort of central organization as the Catholic hierarchy, nor the same sort of political clout—to test the emergency orders in court. Indeed, some leading prelates went out of their way to promote the emergency orders. New Jersey's Governor Phil Murphy told an interviewer that he had coordinated his plans with Cardinal Joseph Tobin of Newark, to be sure that priests in his state would not be permitted to hold drive-in Communion services.

In California, Rev. John MacArthur, pastor to a huge Evangelical congregation, took the opposite approach. He challenged a ban in court, characterizing the order as "a direct ban on engaging in the worship which our faith requires." His declaration in court remarked that the ban would "take the position that we should lock our doors and force our congregants to gather to worship the Lord in parking lots, in parks, or perhaps beaches—but never in any church." That requirement, he bluntly affirmed, was "nonsensical."

Halfway around the globe, the leading figure in the Orthodox world, Patriarch Bartholomew of Constantinople, balked at government directives, saying that it was "impossible for us to remain silent in the face of such an ambiguous situation." Although he does not have the protection of a constitutional guarantee like the First Amendment and, in fact, lives in a nation (Turkey) where Islamic political power is on the rise, the Ecumenical Patriarch stated that the Orthodox Church could not submit "to the authorities of this world when the Divine Eucharist is called into question."

Contagious Faith

Archbishop Cordileone's Campaign

In the United States, the prelate who was most vocal in questioning unreasonable government regulations was Archbishop Salvatore Cordileone of San Francisco. But even he stopped short of a court challenge. He rallied public support for the Church, telling the faithful that city officials "are mocking you, and even worse, they are mocking God," with emergency rules that put tighter restrictions on Catholic churches than on tattoo parlors. He collected more than 17,000 signatures on a petition "asking the City of San Francisco to free the Mass." He held public rallies and—when the city proclaimed that no more than one hundred people could attend even an outdoor Mass in a public plaza—he scheduled four Masses simultaneously outside the city's cathedral to allow for a larger number of congregants. But he did not directly defy the city's rules.

The Church counsels Catholics to respect legitimate authority and obey duly constituted laws. But during the lockdown, the oppressive restrictions were established not by law but by regulatory orders, issued by civic officials whose authority to make such rules was at best questionable. And even if the orders were legal, the Church teaches that unjust laws do not command our obedience. In fact the *Catechism of the Catholic Church* goes further: "The citizen is *obliged in conscience not to follow* the directives of civil authorities when they are contrary to the demands of the moral order, to the fundamental rights of persons or the teachings of the Gospel" (emphasis added). What could be more directly contrary to the demands of the moral order than a draconian restriction on the celebration of the Eucharist, the "source and summit" of our spiritual life? What could be more clearly contrary to the teachings of the Gospel than a regulation that is a "mockery of God?"

When I questioned Archbishop Cordileone as to why he did not simply ignore the restrictions, invite the faithful into his cathedral, and celebrate Mass, he replied that such an action "would have been seen as reckless." The city's regulations were welcomed by many of the people of San Francisco, he remarked—including many Catholics frightened by the virus. If he defied the restrictions, political leaders would have condemned him for endangering the public, thus strengthening public opinion in their favor and making it even harder to win a political campaign against the restrictions.

When I pressed the question of civil disobedience and suggested that the arrest of an archbishop might swing public opinion toward his cause, Archbishop Cordileone indicated that he would not be afraid to risk arrest. "Oh, if I thought that's what would happen, I'd do it," he said. But he feared that city officials would *not* arrest him—that instead they would find other, subtler ways to punish the church, such as imposing fines on small, vulnerable parishes. On the broader question of civil disobedience, he said: "I don't perceive a need now, but I'm taking no options off the table."

A few weeks later Archbishop Cordileone proclaimed victory in his publicity campaign, when the city raised the limit on indoor worship to allow one hundred people at a Mass—which at the time matched the maximum allowed by the state of California. Thus the San Francisco archdiocese was released from one absurd and unfair local regulation but still bound by an absurd and unfair state rule.

Archbishop Cordileone chose to bring his fight to the court of public opinion, and he won at least a limited victory. But public opinion shifts constantly and responds most readily to influences that are not at all friendly to the Catholic Church. When the next confrontation came (and could anyone doubt that it was coming?) government officials could say to Church leaders: "You accepted the state restrictions; why can't you accept these few new rules?" Eventually the issue would have to be tested: not in the court of public opinion but in a court of law.

One Diocese Dares a Court Challenge

Bishop Nicholas DiMarzio of Brooklyn chose a legal option, joining with several synagogues to challenge tight restrictions in New York. The case went to the U.S. Supreme Court, where the religious leaders won a landmark victory; the court ruled that emergency orders could not impose tighter restrictions on religious worship than on other similar activities. In a fiery opinion, concurring with the majority decision, Justice Neil Gorsuch went to the heart of the issue:

> It is time— past time—to make plain that, while the pandemic poses many grave challenges, there is no world in which the Constitution tolerates color-coded executive edicts that reopen liquor stores and bike shops but shutter churches, synagogues, and mosques.

The Supreme Court decision set a precedent that other federal courts were bound to follow, thus opening the door for other dioceses to file the same sort of challenge and expect the same sort of result. When the Archdiocese of Washington, D.C.—evidently emboldened by the success of the Brooklyn diocese—launched a challenge against special restrictions in that city, the mayor quickly backed down and agreed to end the discriminatory treatment of churches.

The Brooklyn diocese won a very important victory in this case. Especially so, because the Supreme Court decision included a warning to government officials that they could not skirt the impact of the ruling by easing their emergency restrictions *after* a suit had been filed. The mere threat of a legal challenge was now enough to deter civil leaders from making overly restrictive rules. Yet even after the Supreme Court handed religious groups this powerful defensive weapon, few American dioceses chose to use it. Most dioceses had declined to challenge restrictions; that passive attitude endured.

More than that, many American dioceses and archdioceses had made it virtually impossible to mount legal challenges against government restrictions because their bishops and archbishops had made a point of saying that they were releasing special rules for their churches on their own authority, not because of orders from governors or mayors. It was purely coincidental, we were asked to believe, that the bishop's orders just happened to match the orders from civic leaders in every particular. When a Catholic layman in Massachusetts brought suit against his governor for restricting his freedom to worship, a federal court rejected his suit, observing quite accurately: "There is no evidence, however, that the archdiocese instituted its protocols only because of Governor Baker's orders."

A governor's restrictions on churches can be appealed in a court of law. A bishop's orders cannot. When the bishop issues orders to his pastors, and those orders match the governor's emergency restrictions, the bishop is thereby insulating the governor from the possibility of legal challenge.

Facing Tough Choices

In France, Bishop Joseph Ginoux of Montauban suggested that bishops needed the support (and perhaps the prodding) of the laity to steel their resolve. "It's easy to ask bishops to take the lead if no one stands behind them," he reasoned. He suggested that lay Catholics should "invade the churches at Mass times, ask for the Mass, and bishops and priests will come to celebrate it." That tactic sounds reasonable enough, but there are practical difficulties. Which churches should the people invade? What *are* the Mass times? Or should the lay faithful make those decisions for themselves: choose a church and a time, assemble, and wait and pray for a willing priest?

That route could be revealing in another way. Bishops and priests would be shown, in very dramatic fashion, that some Catholics were willing to make sacrifices — even perhaps to risk arrest — in order to receive the sacraments. They would know, in other words, which Catholics are most dedicated to their faith. Perhaps that knowledge would help Church leaders to adjust the balance of their scales, weighing the demands of the faithful hungry for the sacraments more heavily than those of Catholics anxious to comply with secular authorities.

Sooner or later Church leaders must make some difficult decisions. Many Catholics are fearful of contracting the virus and therefore ready to justify even the most draconian restrictions on public life, including the life of the Church. How far can their worries be accommodated without endangering the rights of the faith and the integrity of Catholic sacramental life? Or to pose the question differently: Are the restrictions imposed on the Church because of the Covid epidemic reasonable and just? Are the restrictions necessary to protect public health? Or do they unduly burden the free exercise of religion?

A Question of Motivations

Early on in the lockdown, Michael Pakaluk published a perceptive essay in *The Catholic Thing* calling attention to the ideological predilections of the secular leaders who were guiding our society toward isolation. He invited readers to cast their minds back just a few months, to December 2019, and think about the motivations that guided some of the "best and brightest" in our society before the epidemic was in the headlines. Think about the powerful people who believed that:

- the human race is a blight, a danger to the earth's delicate ecosystem;
- population control should be our highest public priority;
- inequality is always wrong, and wealth should be redistributed;
- the economic marketplace is driven by greed alone;
- private individuals cannot be trusted to make the right decisions; government programs are more reliable; and
- staying alive and healthy is the ultimate good; there's nothing more important beyond this life.

Should we trust these experts to make the decisions that could dramatically alter the course of our lives and the shape of our society? Pakaluk added another very important question: Shouldn't we notice that someone who holds the opinions sketched above would have a strong inclination to continue the national shutdown indefinitely? Several months later—as politicians argued that because the lockdown had not yet eradicated the virus, there must be a much more stringent lockdown—his essay appears prophetic.

The ideological bias of the lockdown became unavoidably apparent when government officials who had insisted that public meetings were dangerous welcomed the mass demonstrations by supporters of Black Lives Matter, a movement with a hard-left orientation. It was still more obvious when Dr. Anthony Fauci, the federal government's leading exponent of the lockdown, pointedly refused to condemn casual sexual encounters, instead giving the anodyne advice that anyone interested in the hookup culture should be careful. In New York—both the city and the state—chief government executives singled out Jewish communities for enforcement measures, sending chills of recognition through anyone conscious of twentieth-century history. And in state after state, abortion clinics were classified as "essential," but churches were not. The lockdown was not neutral. Some causes were favored over others; some gatherings were immune from criticism while others were special targets.

In Massachusetts, during the summertime prime season of the Black Lives Matter rallies, Governor Charlie Baker encouraged anyone who had participated in a "large public gathering" to be tested for the coronavirus. By "large public gathering" of course he meant the Black Lives Matter demonstrations: the only large gatherings that had been allowed in Massachusetts recently. The tests were to be free: that is, they would be administered at public expense, and the results would be confidential.

No such special arrangements were available to people who did *not* attend the Black Lives Matter rallies. Someone who had gone to Mass the last Sunday or visited Grandma in a nursing home, and now was worried about a persistent cough, could be tested—at his own expense. The results would not be confidential. If his test were positive for the virus, a team of contact tracers would require him to furnish a list of everyone he had met recently.

In New York, Governor Cuomo went a step further, instructing contact tracers that they should not ask those pesky questions of anyone who has been at a Black Lives Matter event. Everyone else was expected to provide public health officials with a list of all their friends; left-wing activists would be exempt. This clearly political decision meant that the entire contact-tracing effort would be a sham, since the likeliest sources of infection—the events that might be classified as "super-spreaders"—would not be included in the statistics.

Contact Tracing

Yet through it all, prominent Catholic leaders were enthusiastic supporters of the lockdown measures. Pastors went online to advertise the extraordinary measures they had taken to comply with—and even exceed!—the most stringent measures public health officials had put in place.

Catholic parishes and dioceses enthusiastically joined in the contact-tracing campaign. Pastors recruited volunteers to take down the names of the parishioners who showed up for Mass or for confession. Being required to register by name for Mass is an affront; being required to give one's name before making a sacramental confession is a violation of the right to an anonymous encounter. But these practices became common in many dioceses.

Pastors explained that registering for a place at Mass was a necessity, since their churches could not exceed the prescribed limit for the congregation. But if public health officials determined that a Covid-positive individual had attended Mass, the parish would be under heavy pressure to surrender the list to the contact-tracers. Given their track record, there was no reason to doubt that the parishes would quickly hand over those lists, and everyone who was present at the same Mass would be ordered to quarantine for fourteen days. In some more extreme cases, parish volunteers waited at the church doors and admitted only the parishioners they recognized: a flagrant rejection of the principle that anyone should be welcome at a Catholic church and, thus, a gross setback for the cause of evangelization. But evangelization—that is, inviting people *into* the church—was definitely not a top priority in the Covid era.

Ethical Questions on Vaccines

When would this awful epidemic end? When could the Church resume her normal life of prayer and public witness? For months, public health officials held out the promise that an effective vaccine could curb the epidemic and allow a restoration of normal life. (By the time the vaccines first became available, toward the very end of 2020, the public health czars had withdrawn that promise. The vaccines alone would not end the epidemic, they admitted; the emergency restrictions would have to remain in place for months.) Quite understandably, then, many Church leaders joined in the general clamor for a vaccine.

But there was a catch. Many vaccines—for Covid or for other diseases—are produced using tissue lines taken from abortions. Many others use the fetal tissues in testing their products. Anyone who used those vaccines became involved, however remotely, in the abortion industry. Should Catholics accept a vaccine with that provenance or—assuming that they wanted a Covid vaccine—hold out for an ethically acceptable alternative?

In July, the bishops of the United Kingdom surrendered on that question, even before the battle had properly begun. Worse, they gave up what was not theirs to give: the rights of the faithful.

In a statement that purported to give "The Catholic Position on Vaccination," the Bishops' Conference of England and Wales asserted that Catholics have "a prima facie duty to be vaccinated" and a "moral obligation to guarantee the vaccination coverage necessary for the sake of others." Immediately, any shrewd observer knew that when a Covid vaccine became available, that statement by the English bishops would be quoted

by zealous lawmakers campaigning to make the vaccine mandatory—and thus to deprive the English people of the freedom
to make their own medical decisions for themselves and for
their children.

In fact, the bishops' statement itself was clearly an argument
in favor of vaccination—perhaps even mandatory vaccination.
The bishops were determined to rally Catholics to that cause.
In a release accompanying the statement, the bishops' conference said that its goal is "to encourage Catholics to commit to
protecting the most vulnerable in society"—by vaccination,
naturally. There was no Covid vaccine currently available, so
this statement was preparing the ground in advance: clearing
away possible opposition before the inevitable rush to vaccinate.

Some of the vaccines currently being developed at the time
derived from fetal cells obtained in abortions. Were the English
bishops ignoring the ethical questions involved? Not quite. The
document conceded: "The Church is opposed to the production of vaccines using tissue derived from aborted fetuses, and
we acknowledge the distress many Catholics experience when
faced with a choice of not vaccinating their child or seeming to
be complicit in abortion."

The "distress" that "some" Catholics experience: that was
a nice way of minimizing the gravity of a real moral problem.
But—you can feel the "but" coming, can't you?—the English
bishops were not going to let that moral problem deter them.
The statement went on:

> Nevertheless, the Church teaches that the paramount
> importance of the health of a child and other vulnerable
> persons could permit parents to use a vaccine which was
> in the past developed using these diploid cell lines.

So the "paramount importance" of vaccination outweighed the "distress" that "some" Catholics might feel. Even if the first Covid vaccine that emerged from the current competition was unethically derived, the logic of the English bishops insisted that the faithful should accept it.

Conflicting Directives

In reaching that conclusion, the bishops' statement cited a 2005 directive from the Pontifical Academy for Life, which said that "all clinically recommended vaccinations can be used with a clear conscience." But they neglected another sentence from that same Vatican document, in which the Pontifical Academy said that "there remains a moral duty to continue to fight and to employ every lawful means in order to make life difficult for the pharmaceutical industries which act unscrupulously and unethically."

The way to "make life difficult" for unethical pharmaceutical corporations would be to fight strenuously against the development and approval of any vaccine developed from fetal cell lines. The time to object to unethical vaccines was *before* any vaccine was approved for use. By signaling so clearly that they would support the use of *even an unethical vaccine*, the English bishops surrendered before that battle had begun in earnest.

Worse, the bishops' statement undercut the witness of those Catholics (and non-Catholics) who would refuse an unethical vaccine. The Pontifical Academy had acknowledged the evangelical value of that witness in 2005. More recently, Helen Watt of the Anscombe Bioethics Centre explained:

> Even if there is no absolute duty to boycott vaccines
> produced via existing foetal cell-lines—this is a matter

for individual conscience and there will often be weighty reasons against it—some will feel, whether rightly or wrongly, called to a boycott even if no alternative vaccine is available to them.

If a Covid vaccine developed from fetal cell lines were to be developed, approved, and mandated in the United Kingdom, consider the position of the Catholics who resisted the mandate, in light of the bishops' statement. They would now be told that they were simply wrong: that the Catholic Church does not support their ethical choice. They would be under pressure—perhaps even ordered by the government—to do something they considered morally repugnant, and their bishops would be cited to support that mandate.

And by the way, that entire argument presupposed that a Covid vaccine would work effectively to prevent the disease. Since the coronavirus acted much like a flu, and flu vaccines are notoriously unable to guarantee immunity, there was always ample reason for skepticism on that score. Were the bishops saying that good Catholics should take the vaccine even if it might not work? And what about undesirable side effects? Were Catholics morally bound to take a vaccine—and give their young children a vaccine—even if it was potentially harmful and not certainly effective?

Not all vaccines are alike. Some pharmaceutical companies have used fetal tissues in the production of their vaccines. Other companies have used the fetal tissues to develop and test their products, but those tissue lines are not included in the actual vaccines.

Among the first vaccines available on the American market, the AstaZenaca and Johnson & Johnson vaccines, use the aborted fetal tissues in production. The Moderna and Pfizer vaccines do not include the fetal cells, but they were tested on fetal-tissue lines. (The Charlotte Lozier Institute and Children of God for Life both maintain sites that list the vaccines being developed and their connection—if any—with the use of fetal tissues.) From a Catholic moral perspective, the AstraZeneca and Johnson & Johnson vaccines are clearly objectionable. To use them is to become involved in a causal chain that began with an abortion. To be sure, the abortions took place long ago, and it is an exaggeration to say that a dose of these vaccines will contain cells from those unborn babies. (The cells in the vaccine are *derived* from the fetal cells.) Still, the use of the vaccine entails cooperation in abortion.

Because this cooperation is remote and unintentional—what moralists call *passive material cooperation*, many Catholic moralists argue that the use of such vaccines could be justified if there is a grave reason and no alternative is available. In 2008 the Congregation for the Doctrine of the Faith issued a statement backing that argument. And in December 2020, as the first Covid vaccines became available, the Vatican concluded that the use of these vaccines could be justified in cases of grave necessity if no alternatives were available.

That December 2020 statement, issued by the Congregation for the Doctrine of the Faith, conceded that the Vatican did not have the medical and scientific knowledge to determine whether the Covid vaccines would be safe or effective. Nevertheless, the Congregation did say that the Covid epidemic constituted the sort of "grave necessity" that could justify the use of an ethically tainted vaccine.

This new Vatican statement went well beyond the more cautious reasoning expressed in 2005 by the Pontifical Academy for Life, in an extended answer to questions about childhood vaccinations. That earlier statement said that "it is right to abstain from using these vaccines if it can be done without causing children, and indirectly the population as a whole, to undergo significant risks to their health."

More recently, John Haas, the former president of the National Catholic Bioethics Center, accurately summarized the directives from Rome: "The Vatican repeatedly stated that Catholics have an obligation to protest the use of these vaccines if, for a grave reason, they receive it."

Notice that key phrase: "for a grave reason." The Catholic bishops of England and Wales had pronounced that there was indeed a grave reason to take a Covid vaccine; later, the Vatican's Congregation for the Doctrine of the Faith reached the same conclusion. But even that judgment did not constitute a justification for taking *any* Covid vaccine. If one vaccine is developed from fetal tissues and another from ethically acceptable materials, the moral obligation to avoid the former vaccine remains in place.

The bishops of Alberta and the Northwest Territories offered more nuanced moral guidance, saying that it may be justifiable to take the tainted vaccines. But they added: "It remains imperative that Catholics make clear their moral objection to vaccine development derived from abortion, and to advocate with their governments for ethically produced vaccines." If such ethically produced vaccines become available, they would clearly be preferred.

And what about the Moderna and Prizer vaccines, which do not include fetal tissue cells but have been developed and/or tested with fetal tissues? The Moderna vaccine involves a particularly complicated sequence: it was developed using a "spike protein" that had been produced by a different company, using fetal cells. Moderna was not involved in the development of that spike cell, and fetal tissues were not used in the development of the Moderna vaccine. Still, both the Moderna and Pfizer vaccines are connected, however loosely, to the abortion that originally produced those cell lines.

In a joint statement issued in November, the chairmen of the U.S. bishops' committees on doctrine and on pro-life affairs agreed that the Pfizer and Moderna vaccines "are not completely free from any connection to abortion." However, the bishops observed, the connection is "relatively remote." They concluded:

> Some are asserting that if a vaccine is connected in any way with tainted cell lines, then it is immoral to be vaccinated with them. This is an inaccurate portrayal of Catholic moral teaching.

Here it is important to remember that the bishops are addressing the morality of the Moderna and Pfizer vaccines, and not the AstraZeneca and Johnson & Johnson vaccines, which are more closely connected to abortion. In a case of grave need, *remote* material cooperation may be justified. Even in such cases, the 2005 Vatican statement reminds Catholics that they have other moral options:

> They should take recourse, if necessary, to the use of conscientious objection with regard to the use of vaccines produced by means of cell lines of aborted human fetal origin. Equally, they should oppose by all means (in writing, through various associations, mass media, etc.) the vaccines which do not yet have morally acceptable alternatives, creating pressure so that alternative vaccines are prepared, which are not connected with the abortion

of a human fetus, and requesting rigorous legal control of the pharmaceutical industry producers.

The Difficulty of Resistance

Realistically, how would lay Catholics register their moral objections to a vaccine once it had been introduced? Doctors do not ordinarily give their patients a choice of vaccines; if the patient wants the vaccine, the doctor administers what he has. If the patient does protest, at that point the doctor nods his head; the message does not reach the pharmaceutical company that produced the vaccine, nor the government agencies that approved it. The only effective resistance against immoral vaccines would come *before* they are available. For the Covid vaccine, regrettably, that time has already passed.

Still there remains the possibility that a cadre of dedicated Catholics, doggedly resisting even remote cooperation with the abortion industry, will refuse to take vaccines that are unethically derived. With their refusal, they will be making a strong public witness to the integrity of human life. They (I should say "we" because I will be in that camp) can only hope that their bishops do not stifle that witness by falsely suggesting that the vaccines carry no moral taint.

Laypeople ready to take a firm stand, Church leaders counseling them to hold back; lay faithful ready to sacrifice, bishops telling them that the sacrifice is unnecessary: these are familiar themes of Catholic life in recent decades. Pro-life Catholics have gone to jail for their cause, firmly believing that in doing so they were serving their faith. Their bishops did not repudiate them—but (with rare exceptions) did not join them or even endorse them, either. So today zealous Catholics do not really expect their bishops to defy government orders to stay away from Mass or even peer pressure to take a tainted vaccine. Our expectations have been tamped down; we will be satisfied if our bishops do not actively oppose our witness.

Responsible Church leaders want to shield their people from suffering. But should they discourage them from making voluntary sacrifices? They want to protect the physical health of their flocks. But should they lock out Catholics who are willing to take risks for the sake of the sacraments? The bishops understandably worry about public opinion, and in a time of hysterical fear about the Covid virus, it is true that anyone who opposes government emergency regulations can become the target of public animosity. But Christians have faced hostility and outright persecution often in the past, and while the conflict has been painful, the results have invariably included a rebirth of Christian evangelization. To sacrifice vigorous Christian life for the sake of community standing is to ensure that the Church will lose *both* her vigor *and* her standing.

Nevertheless, in 2020, all over the United States, bishops accepted government restrictions on the life of the Church — or, as we have seen, imposed their own restrictions to match or even to exceed the government orders. A precedent has been set; a radical and dangerous step has been taken. Among the propositions explicitly condemned by Pope Pius IX in his *Syllabus of Errors* was the notion that a civil authority "has the right to make enactments regarding the administration of the divine sacraments, and the dispositions necessary for receiving them." Civil leaders erroneously exercised that "right" in 2020, claiming the authority to govern religious activities.

"No greater proof that religion belongs to the State is required than the decree that Christmas is cancelled this year, just as Easter was," wrote Douglas Farrow in *Catholic World Report*. "Indeed, depending on where you live, it may be cancelled in your home as well as in your parish. In some provincial and state jurisdictions you are not to open your banqueting table to guests of any description." Farrow went on:

> So what now? Are we to combine anarchism, you ask, with alarmism? Is it a rebellion we are after? No. Civil disobedience in recognition of the superiority of the law of God over the law of man is not rebellion. It is not another Peasants' Revolt I am advocating, but rather a united and determined civil disobedience of the kind we know well from the days of Martin Luther King Jr., this time in defense of the *libertas ecclesia* and of religious freedom more broadly.

David Warren, writing for *The Catholic Thing*, echoed the message: "This is what I hope my fellow Catholics will do. Go to Mass and, if someone tries to stop us, make them physically prevent it. For cowardice is not a Catholic virtue."

The Risk of Worship

In justifying special restrictions on churches, governors and mayors have claimed that church services are particularly dangerous as occasions for the transfer of the Covid virus. It is true that a few famous outbreaks of the disease have been traced to church meetings. But invariably these have been small churches, in which the congregation was tightly packed for a lengthy service: not the description of an ordinary Catholic parish. In fact, as I write, eight months after the lockdown began, not a single case of Covid transmission has been traced back to a Catholic church in the United States.

Yet in one sense civic leaders are right to think of churches as their greatest challenge—not as a challenge to public health but as a challenge to ambitious politicians who seek greater power. The Church has always been a brake on arrogant politicians, a limit to their claims of authority, because the Church asserts an authority that is higher than—and prior to—the authority of the state. The state has power over one's life; the Church teaches that life (on this earth) is not one's highest good.

"If we accept Hobbes's thesis that the city of men is founded on the fear of death, religion is intrinsically dangerous," wrote the French political philosopher Rémi Brague. The Church points toward a force more powerful than the Leviathan, commanding more loyalty than the state. A healthy and vigorous Church should not be any threat to a limited government, but when political leaders overstep their bounds, the battle is joined.

And when that battle is joined and Church leaders do not defend the borders of their own proper realm, politicians grow more ambitious. "My worry," wrote Douglas Farrow, "is that by their compliance they are endorsing, or will be seen to be endorsing, not the Gospel of the Kingdom but the gospel of the state; that they are making the priorities of the state their own, rather than the priorities of Jesus."

If Catholic bishops are seen as endorsing the priorities of the state, then those doughty Christians who resist the secular power will be more vulnerable to political repercussions, more vulnerable to public pressure, more vulnerable to the growing hostility of the secular world. Sooner or later, the Church must resist the Leviathan. The contest is coming—indeed it has already begun. The question is whether loyal Catholics will join the struggle now or stand by as observers until their numbers are smaller and their strength further sapped.

8

Fear Itself

When I read the news headline in August, it suddenly all seemed clear. The story reported that new positive Covid tests were attributed to "community spread." Well, of course! That's how contagious diseases are contracted, is it not? They spread through the community. But this is the first time, in our long history of fighting diseases, that we have sought to stop the spread of a contagious disease by abolishing the community.

The phenomena of social distancing, of wearing masks, of viewing every passing neighbor as a threat, of closing down shops and schools and churches, and so on — all these steps have been destructive to our communal life. But most Americans have been willing to accept the anomic terms of the lockdown, with our opinion-makers exhorting us to accommodate ourselves to a "new normal." Why is that? I suggest that in the Western world today many people, especially among the elites, are quite willing to forfeit community life, while others are actively working to destroy it. We are witnessing — perhaps even unthinkingly participating in — the suicide of our culture.

The harshest critics of contemporary Western culture, who believe that selfish individuals are responsible for the destruction of our ecosystem, were quick to embrace the plan to shut down our economy, our schools and churches, our social lives. They persistently ignore the enormous social and economic costs of the shutdown because, to their way of thinking, those costs could actually be benefits.

So now millions of people are unemployed and millions more are desperately lonely and bored and depressed; the rates of suicide and drug abuse and domestic violence have soared; diseases *other* than Covid are being undiagnosed and untreated; violence and mob rule are spreading through the cities; and the social life of an entire society — the family gatherings, the children playing, the young couples dating and marrying, the parties and games and concerts — is on hold indefinitely. All this is unfortunate by any reckoning. But it may seem less tragic — it may even seem a price worth paying — if you have no love for our society's economic and social life, no love for our culture.

Pope St. John Paul II was the great diagnostician of the "culture of death." He showed us how the uglier trends in the Western world — the legalization of abortion, the breakdown in marriages, the trend toward euthanasia, the acceptance of aberrant sexuality — were produced by a steady erosion of respect for human life. By embracing contraception and divorce, our society first severed the link between sex and procreation, then invented the fiction that a permanent union can be broken without disastrous consequences. More or less deliberately, we lost the sense that we are related to our great-great-grandparents and our great-great grandchildren — that we *owe* something to both the ancestors we never met and the progeny we will never see.

"May you see your children's children!" says the psalmist (128:6). The force of that joyful wish — preserved in the beautiful blessing for a Catholic wedding ceremony — is lost on a culture that thinks of children as incidental to marriage (they may or may not come, may or may not be welcome) and has trouble sorting out, after two or three generations of mix-and-match unions, which children belong to which lineage. When you no longer feel that your children are a *part* of you and you are a part of your parents, you become an autonomous individual.

The culture of death has exalted that autonomy, elevating individual choice to become society's highest value. A person's choice is prized more highly than truth, and so a man is allowed to proclaim that he is a woman, despite the clear scientific evidence to the contrary. Choice ranks higher than life itself, and so the law now sanctions a man's choice to end his own life. Justice Anthony Kennedy (who, by the way, identified himself as Catholic) gave full voice to this attitude, and elevated it to the level of Constitutional principle. Writing for the Supreme Court majority in the 1992 *Casey* decision, which upheld the *Roe v. Wade* precedent and preserved access to abortion on demand, Justice Anthony Kennedy made an astonishing claim: "At the heart of liberty is the right to define one's own concept of existence, of meaning, of the universe, and of the mystery of human life."

The Freedom of Isolation

Is that the ultimate goal in life: to be a free-floating individual, making up one's own reality? If Justice Kennedy is right, then my liberty is threatened whenever anyone questions my understanding of existence. By that logic, there can be no tragedy worse than being deprived of the opportunity to make my own choices. I must be free to break any commitments, to alter any circumstances, that hold me back. I cannot acknowledge any debt to society or even to my family. I must be free.

And one more thing: I must be healthy. I cannot tolerate the risk of disease. So, when an epidemic strikes (as epidemics occasionally do, from time to time through history), I must do everything possible to protect myself, and *you* must do everything possible, too, to protect me. There is nothing more important, to me and to you, than staying alive.

That notion would be foreign to our ancestors, who had little choice but to accept the risk of illness and early death. It would be foreign, too, to all the people we regard as heroes, who willingly accepted greater risks for greater causes. In fact, it is foreign to something fundamental in human nature. We take on risks every day; to risk nothing is to accomplish nothing.

So why, when this epidemic broke out, did we so quickly accept the notion that the normal functioning of our society was not worth the risk? The answer to that question has gradually become clear.

The first clue came when Dr. Anthony Fauci, the chief arbiter of acceptable risk (and another Catholic), declined to condemn anonymous sexual encounters, even at the height of the pandemic. "You know, that's tough," he said, when asked about casual sexual encounters, "because that's what's called relative risk." A "relative risk" for the sake of fleeting gratification—for an individual's irresponsible choice—was somehow less dangerous to the public weal than a normal business transaction or a family funeral.

The next clue, a much more conclusive one, came when Dr. Fauci refused to label the massive "Black Lives Matter" protests as a threat to public health, and mayors who had banned other public meetings welcomed demonstrators to their cities. These were clear and obvious violations of "social distancing" rules and quarantine regulations, yet they were tolerated and even applauded. Why?

Now look at what those demonstrations accomplished. When they were peaceful, they were rhetorical attacks on our society's history. When they were violent (as they often were), they resulted in the destruction of private property and public monuments. In other words, one way or another, they tore down what our society has built up.

The public meetings that *build up* our culture — the concerts and parades and lectures and religious rituals — are still banned or tightly restricted. The public events that tend to destroy that culture are allowed, even in flagrant disregard for the reigning emergency regulations. As Yeats put it in "The Second Coming," a poem that might have been written about current events:

> The best lack all conviction, while the worst
> Are full of passionate intensity.

By pulling down statues of explorers and war heroes, violent leftists show their contempt for our history. But they will not stop there because the veneration of historical figures, while it is a noble display of *pietas*, is not the ultimate basis for a healthy culture. Far more important is the *cult* itself: the veneration of almighty God. So it should be no surprise that, having first taken aim at Civil War monuments, the vandals next set their sights on churches — specifically Catholic churches. If your most cherished objective is to be free of all restraints — if your battle cry is *"Non serviam!"* — you have ample reason to see the Church as your foe.

Archbishop Cordileone recognized the problem in San Francisco when, after rioters tore down a statue of St. Junipero Serra, he conducted an exorcism at the parish where the outrage occurred. The vandalism had not been just another display of misplaced anger, he realized; something more insidious was at work. The forces arrayed against the Catholic Church are growing steadily stronger and bolder; the civilizing influences of a once-Christian culture no longer restrain them.

The question that remains is whether the Church, the People of God, will recognize the danger and mobilize before the active persecution begins and our culture is "cancelled."

The Limits of Safety

Does it seem hyperbolic to say that seemingly mild public health measures—masks, social distancing, restrictions on commerce—are assaults on our civilization? Perhaps so. Since time immemorial, prudent people have taken steps to avoid contagion during epidemics. But never before have those steps been mandated on a national, even global, scale. Individuals and families made their own choices, took their own risks, according to their own priorities.

When government officials set blanket policies, they cannot possibly anticipate every individual's needs. The policies that seem reasonable to one person or group will seem outrageous to some other people, and to still others, they will be impossible to fulfill. Since I work alone in a comfortable office, the order to wear a mask in public places causes me very little inconvenience. For someone who works long hours on a hot and crowded factory floor, it is a distinct hardship. A large corporation with a cushion of capital can endure a year of depressed sales; a mom-and-pop shop will go bankrupt, crushing a family's dreams. A healthy man can postpone a cancer screening, but if it turns out that he was not healthy—that the cancer was beginning to grow—the missed appointment might cost him his life. A young couple can postpone their planned anniversary trip abroad, but an elderly woman might not live to see her newborn grandchild.

How can we fine-tune the restrictions, to allow exceptions for exceptional cases? We cannot. Individuals can make their own decisions; governments cannot weigh their needs for them.

Accepting Risks

In the wake of a devastating hurricane in Louisiana a few years ago, my friend Brian, who works for a utility company, joined a crew that traveled to the stricken region to help. For a week they devoted long overtime hours to restore power to the victims' homes. Working on power lines, often at night and in rough weather, is dangerous. Although these experienced workers knew their business, they also knew that a careless mistake—all the more likely when they were overtired—could be fatal. Yet they did the job; they had volunteered for just this work.

And what did those linemen accomplish? When electricity was restored, some families did nothing more important than relax with inane television shows. But in other cases, the electric power meant that precious food would not go bad and families would have enough to eat, medicine would retain its potency, or disabled people could recharge their wheelchairs. The streetlights that had gone dark were on again, easing the flow of traffic—perhaps preventing serious accidents. Medical clinics could resume normal operation. Brian and his colleagues could not anticipate every use of the power they were restoring, nor could they distinguish between the "essential" and "non-essential" uses of electricity. They worked to restore power to everyone, to enable a way of life that included both the sublime and the ridiculous. And notice: to enable that way of life, they risked their lives.

Is it sensible—is it right—to risk one's life to defend a way of life? That question has arisen more than once in this book. The truth is that we do take risks, every day, because of our way of life: whenever we drive a car, use a power tool, climb a staircase, drink a cocktail, or go for a swim. Life can be dangerous; we take our chances.

The Price of Life

On one hand, it would be callous to put a price on a human life: to suggest that we would accept X amount of inconvenience in order to save Y number of lives. But as a matter of fact, we do make such decisions, more or less unconsciously, on a regular basis. Moreover, some hardheaded professionals, such as actuaries in insurance companies and lawyers handling wrongful-death suits, do make an effort to put a price on the value of an additional year of life.

The actuarial statistics cannot be applied to the Covid lockdowns, however, for two reasons. First, we cannot begin to calculate all the damage—not only economic but also physical, emotional, and spiritual—done by the extraordinary regulations. Second, we do not know how effective the lockdowns have been in saving lives. That is, if they have been effective at all.

If we could put dollar figures on those losses and gains, would we want to do so? In one of the oddest essays published during this crisis, Matthew Parris wrote in *The Times* of London that we must begin to calculate the costs of safety. "We can, and must, put a price on human life," he wrote. Remarkably, Parris blamed Christianity for the general reluctance to do what he said must be done. Christians, he said, were too much absorbed with saving every life to notice the loss of freedom and normalcy that the lockdown had entailed.

That perspective is exceedingly odd, I would argue, because orthodox Christianity ordinarily has no great fear of death. Yes, every human life is precious. But death is a natural part of life, and while we fight to preserve life, we cannot pretend that anyone has a right to escape death.

In another odd column, Emma Pattee wrote in the *Washington Post* that "Covid-19 makes us think about our mortality. Our brains aren't designed for that." If the human mind is not designed to reflect on mortality, it is remarkable that poets and philosophers have done exactly that for centuries. But Pattee seems to think that their efforts have been unnatural. "Simply put," she wrote, "to function as a conscious being, it's imperative that you be in denial about your impending death."

If that is true, then it follows that the generations of Christians who have meditated on death, who developed the genre of the *memento mori*, are not functioning as conscious beings, at least by Pattee's standards. Here too we see the sharp cleavage between the secular outlook and the Christian faith.

Interestingly enough, one essayist predicted that the Covid epidemic would enable the people of the twenty-first century to look at old works of art with new eyes. Peter Schjeldahl, writing in the *New Yorker*, did not mention the Christian faith that permeated the consciousness of artists in past centuries, but he did raise the pertinent question: "Why does the art of what we term the Old Masters have so much more soulful heft than that of most moderns and nearly all of our contemporaries?" He answered his own rhetorical question: "I think the reason is routine consciousness of mortality."

When art lovers are free to roam through museums again, Schjeldahl predicted, because of the impact of the Covid epidemic, "we will have been reminded of our oneness throughout the world and across time with all the living and the dead." Does that final phrase sound familiar? In the Creed, we Catholics affirm that Christ will come to judge "the living and the dead."

We are all members of the same family. Death does not separate us in the final accounting.

The Certainty of Death

I am going to die.

No, I am not sick. I feel fine. The last time I saw my doctor, he was quite happy with my overall condition. So, I don't mean that I expect to die *soon*—although these days I am acutely aware of that possibility. But even if I continue in good health, at my age I realize that the end is much closer than the beginning. Sooner or later. I shall die. We all do.

That doesn't mean that I take death lightly. When I see death coming (if I see it coming), I don't suppose I'll be so philosophical about it. I don't want to die. My plan is to "live forever or die trying."

Nor do I take it lightly when others die. I have buried and grieved and prayed for my parents, for other relatives and neighbors and friends. I do not expect—do not want—others to "go gentle into that good night." We should all fight against death. These days we are all making substantial sacrifices, for the most part willingly, to preserve not only our own lives but the lives of others—including many that we do not know. As we should.

But even as we make these sacrifices, even as we fight to ward off a deadly epidemic, we should bear in mind two essential truths. First, all of us will die. Every victory over death is only a temporary one. Death is a part of life. Second, there are things worse than death.

A Fate Worse Than Death

What could be worse than death? you might ask. As a Christian, I answer: sin. Far worse than death of the body is death of the soul: separation from God's love, the loss of the unsurpassable eternal reward offered to us through Jesus Christ.

But even if you don't share my faith, even if you are not religious, a similar point can be made. There really *are* fates worse than death. We admire heroes who are willing to give their lives for a noble cause. During the battle of Belleau Wood, a legendary Marine sergeant reportedly exhorted his men to charge by saying, "Come on, you sons of bitches, do you want to live forever?" That's not the sort of language we ordinarily hear in church, but do you notice the similarity of sentiment? There are some things worth dying for.

And, certainly, there are some things worth taking a risk for. As much as we admire bravery in the face of danger, we despise timidity. No doubt you would be safer if you spent your life cowering at home, but what could you accomplish? "A coward dies a thousand times before his death, but the valiant taste of death but once," Shakespeare tells us. To risk nothing is to accomplish nothing.

Are we, as a nation, reaching a point at which our fear of death threatens to paralyze us? Yes, the epidemic justifies extreme measures. But *how* extreme? There may be a point at which we must take risks to preserve both our lives and our very way of life. Will we be ready?

The current restrictions on ordinary life have imposed severe costs, and those costs will multiply as the shutdown lengthens. I do not mean merely economic costs, although those costs can themselves have life-or-death consequences and cannot be ignored. I am thinking rather of the cost to our culture, to our quality of life, to our cohesion as a society. If we are locked down for many more months, as some experts have advised, we may emerge as a very different sort of society.

Political Consequences

Think of the political implications of the restrictions. The First Amendment right to assembly, as well as the right to freedom of worship, have been set aside by emergency orders. Yet the right to assemble (and not only for explicitly political reasons) forms the basis for other rights that we consider fundamental. How can we exercise our rights without gathering? How can we rally to oppose excessive government controls without coming together to discuss our grievances and form our plans?

Self-appointed groups of informers are cropping up to denounce neighbors who are insufficiently obedient to government policies. Local officials are announcing that they will not prosecute petty criminals and will release convicts from prisons. The federal government is proposing to spend trillions of dollars that it does not have, laying huge new burdens of debt on future generations, to prop up a spavined economy. All these developments are dangerous to the future of our republic.

The policies are rationalized — for the short run, at least — by the argument that without them, people will die. But that argument by itself is incomplete because it fails to elaborate on whether the emergency measures will prevent unnecessary deaths. Equally important — and often overlooked — is the likelihood that the shutdown will actually *cause* unnecessary deaths.

To shut down all "nonessential" business is to take an enormous risk — and not only an economic risk. It isn't easy to determine whether or not a business is "essential" to public health. Hospitals need parts and paper and supplies and computer networks. Food must be packaged and shipped and stored. Some work that seems "nonessential" today might become essential later. If you don't replace the brake pads on your car, eventually you may crash. If the building inspector stays home, eventually a fire hazard may cost lives. So people will die: preventable deaths will result from policies that may have been unnecessary.

We are all trying to preserve lives, to preserve the quality and dignity of life. So please don't say that anyone who questions the current draconian restrictions is endangering human lives. Lives are *already* in danger; we are doing our best to save as many as possible.

In time of war, a military commander may be obliged to make a painful choice, knowing full well that any tactic he chooses will endanger lives. Effective leadership entails a willingness to take risks. So it is today, in our war against a deadly virus. Some people will die: that is now a sad but unavoidable reality. We must not allow an inordinate fear of death to stop us from making prudent decisions.

Writing in *Catholic World Report*, Douglas Farrow lamented the emergence of a "health-first heresy" in the Church. "It required no heresiarch to cultivate it other than the human fear of suffering and death," he said. "Its telltale mark is the claim, implicit or explicit, that care for the body trumps care for the soul." This heresy, Farrow continued, is a repudiation of the saints who have built up the Church over the centuries, "because prioritizing disease-prevention over corporate worship of God is no different in principle than prioritizing persecution-prevention over corporate worship of God."

The Catholic Church cannot yield to the health-first heresy, especially not during a crisis like the Covid epidemic. At a time when our entire culture is ridden with anxiety over physical health, the world needs a reminder that we are all mortal, we shall all die—along with the reassurance that Jesus has overcome death. A secular world that sees no hope beyond the grave desperately needs the balm of Christian hope: the sure hope of salvation through Christ's sacrifice. A society paralyzed by fear needs the Church to proclaim boldly—as Jesus taught, as Pope John Paul II frequently repeated—that we must "Be not afraid."

9

Open the Doors and . . .

In March 2020, shortly after the Catholic churches of Rome closed their doors, a note circulated through certain Vatican email accounts: "I think of the people who will certainly abandon the Church when this nightmare is over, because the Church abandoned them when they were in need."

At first a few Vatican journalists mistakenly reported that the note had come from Pope Francis himself. It had not. But it had come from his office: from Msgr. Yoannis Lahzi Gaid, a private secretary to the Pontiff. Now reporters who had played up the story retreated only a bit, saying that such a note would not have been circulated without the Pope's approval. (That assumption was questionable at the time, and the questions were underlined several weeks later, when the Egyptian priest was quietly removed from the pope's personal staff and assigned to new duties in the Secretariat of State.) With or without papal approval, however, the note raised a question that other priests and prelates were asking themselves: When the lockdown ended and the churches reopened, would the Catholic faithful return?

"In the epidemic of fear that we are all living due to the coronavirus pandemic, we risk behaving more like wage-earners than as pastors," Msgr. Gaid wrote.

By September, Cardinal Jean-Claude Hollerich of Luxembourg was resigned to the expectation that Catholic churches in Europe would see a dramatic drop in attendance. The laity, he told the Vatican daily *L'Osservatore Romano*, "have seen that life is very comfortable. They can live very well without having to come to church." The cardinal—who doubles as president of the Commission of Bishops' Conferences of the European Union—predicted a steep drop in baptisms, weddings, and religious instruction. "I am sure of it," he said.

To keep things in proper perspective, Cardinal Hollerich pointed out that the Church had already seen a steady decline in practice over the past few decades. The lockdown was not solely responsible; the number of practicing Catholics would have shrunk in any case, he suggested. "Perhaps it would have taken us ten years longer," but the cardinal saw the negative trend as inevitable.

The same negative trend has been quite evident in the United States. According to figures furnished by Georgetown's Center for Applied Research in the Apostolate (CARA), between 1970 and 2018, the annual number of marriages in Catholic churches fell from 426,309 to 143,087; infant baptisms from 1.089 million to 615,119; students in Catholic elementary and secondary schools from 4.4 million to 1.8 million; and elementary and secondary school students in parish religious education from 5.5 million to 2.9 million. The number of priests dropped from 59,192 to 36,580; religious sisters from 160,931 to 44,117; and the rate of weekly Mass attendance fell from 54.9 percent to 21.1 percent. There was one category that showed a strong upward trend, but it only highlighted the problem: the number of "former Catholic adults" soared from 3.5 million in 1970 to 26.1 million in 2018. In 2019, according to CARA statistics, about 20 percent of Catholic Americans attended Mass on any given Sunday. In 2020, after the Covid lockdown, that figure dropped under 10 percent; only 20 percent of the country's Catholics showed up for Mass on Christmas: the day that ordinarily sees the year's highest church attendance.

The negative trend was unmistakable, certainly. But the Church's response to the Covid crisis did more than simply confirm that trend. For months, bishops and priests assured their people that they could—and probably should—stay home from Mass. They actively discouraged coming to church on Sunday; they told parishioners that watching a livestream liturgy would serve as a perfectly adequate substitute. How could they retract those assurances when the churches opened again? How could they persuade ordinary Catholics that Sunday Mass was a solemn obligation, when they had not offered Sunday Mass for the faithful for months?

For generations, Catholics were taught that they could not eat meat on Fridays under pain of sin. Then after Vatican II, the Church relaxed that discipline, teaching that Catholics could abstain from meat *or* offer some other sacrifice on Fridays instead. The latter part of that message was lost in translation; the vast majority of Catholics now believe that rule of Friday abstinence has simply been abolished. Once the rule was relaxed, in practice it was generally ignored. Does the same fate await the obligation to attend Sunday Mass?

Bishop Thomas Tobin of Providence, Rhode Island, thought it would. "It's clear," he said in August, that on a practical level, "the discipline of attending Sunday Mass is gone. Post-pandemic we'll have to invite people back to Mass by creative outreach." Creative approaches to evangelization are always welcome, but it will take more than a little creativity to recapture the attention of lukewarm Catholics, to impose discipline after telling the world that the discipline is not necessary.

An Inherent Contradiction

During the summer and fall of 2020, as the first wave of the epidemic passed its peak, some American bishops announced that they were ending the dispensation that allowed healthy Catholics to miss Sunday Mass. In Milwaukee, for instance, Archbishop Jerome Listecki announced in September: "Those who deliberately fail to attend Mass commit a grave sin."

Could the archbishop and other prelates expect ordinary Catholics to understand their decisions? Could they expect the faithful to troop back to Sunday Mass after a six-month hiatus? Having used their authority to *stop* lay Catholics from attending Mass, bishops now show a touching confidence in their authority to bring them back. Will this genie go back in the bottle?

"Fear of getting sick, in and of itself, does not excuse someone from the obligation," the archbishop pronounced. But wait: wasn't a fear of illness the reason why Archbishop Listecki and so many other prelates issued a dispensation from that obligation? The archbishop obviously anticipated that question, and his statement continued:

> However, if the fear is generated because of at-risk factors, such as preexisting conditions, age or compromised immune systems, then the fear would be sufficient to excuse from the obligation.

So each lay Catholic would decide for himself whether he had real reason to fear that going to Mass could endanger his health, and if it would not, the regular Sunday obligation would apply. The question would be left to the individual's conscience—as it ordinarily would be left to anyone feeling under the weather to decide whether or not his illness was an adequate excuse to miss Mass.

But the Sunday obligation revived by Archbishop Listecki in September would apply in Milwaukee. What would happen if a lay Catholic who resided in Milwaukee found himself in, say, nearby Chicago on a Sunday morning? Would he still be bound by the Sunday obligation because he was under Archbishop Listecki's authority? Or dispensed because he was in another ecclesiastical jurisdiction where the blanket dispensation was still in place? It is difficult to understand why something that is gravely sinful in one place would not be equally sinful at all just a few miles away.

For that matter, if it would be gravely sinful to skip Mass the next Sunday, why was it acceptable to skip Mass the *last* Sunday? At first glance Archbishop Listecki's decision — and consequently, his warning about the possibility of grave sin — appeared to be based on nothing more than his own personal authority; there was no reference to the Decalogue, to the solemn commandment to keep holy the Lord's Day, to the notion that worship is an obligation in justice.

To an informed Catholic (and bear in mind that not all Catholics are informed), the basic facts are clear:

- The Church, through her hierarchy, has been granted authority by Jesus Christ to impose and lift obligations.
- The Church formally teaches that Mass attendance on Sunday is necessary to fulfill the Third Commandment.
- However, the Church also teaches that the faithful may be excused from this obligation "for a serious reason (for example, illness, the care of infants), or dispensed by their own pastor." A bishop, as pastor for his diocese, thus has authority to issue a blanket dispensation.

What sort of illness constitutes a "serious reason" for failure to attend Sunday Mass? The individual must answer that question for himself. His answer will depend on his particular circumstances: his age, his overall health, his possible risks of exposure to new disease. The pastor cannot come take his temperature and his medical history. The individual must make his own judgment.

Fear of Epidemic, Epidemic of Fear

Back in March, however, the Catholic bishops of the United States—all of them—*did* make that judgment. They decided that *all Catholics* had a "serious reason" for not attending Sunday Mass. That the bishops had the authority to make that judgment, and issue the blanket dispensations, is beyond question. Whether they were *prudent* in doing so is another matter.

When the Covid epidemic first broke upon us, we were virtually all frightened. That fear was not irrational; the disease appeared to be spreading at an objectively frightening rate. The media fanned the flames of fear, and—influenced no doubt by the media hype—so did our bishops. Within weeks all the churches were closed, and for most of us attending Sunday Mass was no longer an obligation; in fact, it was an impossibility.

Bishops are not epidemiologists; they did not know—any more than the rest of us did—how fast the virus would spread and how deadly it would prove. As time passed, more information became available, and we could put the Covid epidemic in perspective, we all reached our own conclusions about the risks we were running and the risks we were prepared to run. But if we concluded that Sunday Mass would be safe—that we no longer had a "serious reason" to absent ourselves—that option still was not open to us because the bishops had closed our churches.

Looking back, Archbishop Listecki explained in his recent statement why the churches were closed:

> As responsible parish communities, we needed to assess the transmission of the Covid-19 virus, permit our parishes the time to establish plans for sanitizing worship spaces, secure needed resources, evaluate the appropriate numbers for social distancing and solicit the voluntary personnel necessary to accomplish the tasks of preparing our worship spaces.

In other words, our bishops and pastors were methodically deciding when and under what conditions *they* thought the churches would be safe. But since bishops have no special expertise on questions of public safety—and since their decisions on this matter were unquestionably based on calculations of public safety—many Catholics were and are likely to question their judgments. Archbishop Listecki acknowledged that a rational fear of exposure to Covid, based on preexisting conditions, "would be sufficient to excuse from the obligation." Just a few weeks earlier the archbishop had effectively ruled that *everyone* had a rational basis for fears. Now he said that, at least for most people, that rational basis is gone. But it isn't that simple. Many Catholics in Milwaukee no doubt *were* still afraid—having been told for months that they should be afraid—and the archbishop could not flip a switch to turn off their fears.

Those fears were amplified when the weather turned cold and the number of new Covid cases began rising once again. Should the bishops who had dispensed the faithful from their Sunday obligation, and then lifted the dispensation, now dispense them once again? And how often could a dispensation be granted before ordinary Catholics began *taking* it for granted?

Bishops can issue authoritative orders, but they cannot flip emotional switches. And when a prelate *seems* to be saying that it is gravely sinful to skip Sunday Mass *because the archbishop says so* — when just last week it wasn't sinful at all *because the archbishop said so* — he is stretching his authority to the breaking point.

Back in March, a number of bishops undermined their own authority still further because they never *did* tell the faithful that they were dispensed from their Sunday Mass obligation; they simply said that there would be no Mass celebrated for the public. Now, of course, the people in that case *were* dispensed, since one is never obligated to do the impossible. But when regular Sunday Mass resumes in those dioceses, it will be very, very difficult for the bishops to insist on the Sunday obligation. It isn't easy to credit a bishop's authority to tell you that you *must* attend Sunday Mass, when he was so ready to announce that you couldn't.

In most American dioceses, Catholics are still dispensed from the Sunday obligation as of the time I am writing in December, nine months after the church doors were closed. But during the summer — at different times in different dioceses — the churches reopened and public celebration of Mass resumed. The congregations were smaller than usual, in part because many people stayed home but also in part because parishes were under orders (from civil and/or ecclesiastical authorities) to limit their congregations to a fraction of their normal seating capacity. Weekly collections were down, too, naturally; a Villanova University study found a 24 percent decline in the average parish. The loss of revenue, coupled with the drop in the number of active parishioners, presaged a different sort of crisis: many parishes would be unable to pay their bills after the crisis ended.

The Traditionalist Surge

Yet there were glimpses of good news for the Church, even in the depths of the Covid calamity. Some pastors went to extraordinary lengths to offer the sacraments, and the faithful flocked to those parishes. Traditionalist communities enjoyed a surge in attendance, as Catholics who were yearning for reverent liturgy found refuge in the Tridentine Mass.

This move toward traditionalism deserves a second look. During the Covid epidemic, Catholics who seek beauty and reverence in the celebration of the Mass faced a new series of worries. Would the new emergency regulations constitute distractions, making it difficult for them to pray? Would there be ugly or even blasphemous variations from the usual ritual? Would their impressionable younger children be given a warped idea of the Mass? As the Covid-era rules changed—sometimes from week to week—they were forced to ask those questions every Sunday morning.

But none of those questions applied to the traditional liturgy, the Catholic Mass as it has been celebrated for centuries: in Latin, with set prayers and carefully prescribed rubrics. The traditional Mass—the "extraordinary form" of the Latin rite, as it was dubbed by Pope Benedict XVI—had not changed following Vatican II and would not change during the Covid epidemic. There would be no intrusive new sanitizing rituals, no new restrictions on the manner of receiving Communion. Catholics who attended Mass at parishes dedicated to the Latin Mass—or at ordinary parishes where the Tridentine liturgy was celebrated once a week—knew what they should expect. There would be no unpleasant surprises, no ugly outcroppings of a fearful attitude alien to Christianity, no concessions to the secular world in the celebration of the transcendent.

Contagious Faith

In this respect, actually, the Covid epidemic accelerated a trend that was already quite visible in Catholicism: the movement of serious Catholics, especially serious *young* Catholics, toward the traditional liturgy. For far too long, orthodox Catholics had been asking those same questions about transcendence and beauty in the liturgy, about irreverence and blasphemy at Mass. Liturgical abuses—some minor, some quite serious—have been commonplace in ordinary Catholic parishes since the 1960s. The Novus Ordo—the form of the Mass that became the norm after Vatican II—allows for multiple variations. Along with the many approved variations, pastors and parish liturgical committees have invented many other possibilities, including more than a few that are at best tasteless, at worst heretical. Any Catholic who has moved from one parish to another or looked for a place to attend Sunday Mass during a vacation trip has experienced the shock of something entirely new and unfamiliar (and perhaps quite unpleasant) in the liturgy. The traditional liturgy offers an oasis from that uncertainty; it will be what it has always been.

It is no coincidence, then, that surveys show the Catholics who are members of traditionalist communities are far more likely than those in conventional parishes to practice their faith regularly, to know and believe what the Church teaches on doctrines of faith (such as the Real Presence in the Eucharist) and on questions of morality (such as abortion and contraception). They have consciously chosen to embrace the Catholic perspective, as opposed to the secular view of the world.

Smaller but More Vigorous

Of course, traditionalists are not the only Catholics who are serious about their faith. In healthy parishes, Catholics who had been starving for the Eucharist showed a new zeal for the Mass when they were invited back into their churches after the first blanket lockdown eased in the summer of 2020. In my own parish I noticed a new development: when the Mass ended, the vast majority of people in the congregation remained for a few minutes, in quiet prayerful thanksgiving, rather than rising from their pews immediately to visit with others, making the church noisy enough so that those who *did* want to pray were distracted.

Overall, the number of Catholics attending Sunday Mass was unquestionably lower. And the drop was not evenly spread across parishes. Healthy parishes saw a substantial decline, but at less active parishes, the congregations dwindled steadily toward extinction. The Covid epidemic had caused or perhaps hastened a winnowing effect, with the most serious and dedicated lay Catholics finding the most serious and dedicated parish communities. (And did I notice an increase in the number attending Mass every weekday?)

The lockdown and its aftermath also had an impact on the home life of serious Catholics, who found themselves more dedicated to family prayer in the absence of parish liturgy. Dedicated lay people found new ways to act out their faith, developing habits of prayer—the family Rosary, the Office of the Hours, singing hymns, reading Scripture—that were likely to endure beyond the end of the epidemic. Is it possible that the lasting impact of the Covid epidemic will be a new appreciation of the universal call to holiness—the long-overdue realization of the Vatican II announcement that this will be the age of the laity?

A Necessary Purgation

We Catholics have all suffered during the Covid epidemic. But the Lord did not promise us an easy life; on the contrary, He promised us suffering. The Covid lockdown has been painful in part because we did not expect it and certainly did not choose it. But we did not choose our own cross. In one of his memorable sermons St. Augustine taught:

> Whenever we suffer some affliction, we should regard it both as a punishment and as a correction. Our holy Scriptures themselves do not promise us peace, security, and rest. On the contrary, the Gospel makes no secret of the troubles and temptations that await us, but it also says that he who perseveres to the end will be saved.

In February, as the Catholic world prepared for Lent, I wrote on my Catholic Culture site:

> So this Lent, my plan is a program of repentance for my own lack of proper reverence for the Eucharist and for the irreverence that has so deeply infected the life of our Church. I encourage other Catholics to join me in that campaign. We can argue later about how to make the liturgy more beautiful, more reverent, more fitting. For now, let's focus on a realization that the first step toward a liturgical revival—which is, necessarily, the first step toward a Catholic spiritual revival—is the recognition that what we *have* been doing is not good enough.

Little did I know, as I wrote those words, that an enforced fast from Communion would increase my longing for the Eucharist, that millions of other Catholics would feel the same longing, that we would come back to our churches with a much deeper appreciation for the beauty of the Mass.

In May, Michael Pakaluk wrote: "A huge opportunity will have been lost if, when the lockdowns end, the lines outside confessionals aren't as impressive as the lines of patrons outside restaurants." Was Pakaluk writing about the repentance that I had in mind back in February? Not quite. But there was (in my mind, at least) a thread of continuity between his column and mine. In both columns—mine, written at a time when a nationwide lockdown was unthinkable; and in his, appearing as the siege was finally beginning to lift—the central focus is on the sense of awe and wonder that we should feel whenever we participate in the holy sacrifice of the Mass.

We human beings are a congenitally ungrateful race, constantly taking the greatest gifts of our Creator for granted. The Old Testament recounts how the Chosen People, again and again, strayed from the path that God had set out for them, up until the arrival of the Messiah. The annals of Church history pick up the story from there. Like spoiled children, we grow tired of God's gifts and look for excitement elsewhere. Manna is a miracle, but when the miracle becomes routine, we long for the fleshpots of Egypt.

Then something happens. Something that brings things back into perspective. Something like the eucharistic famine of the past few months. Suddenly the provision of manna is no longer routine; suddenly attendance at Mass is exceptional. If we are perceptive, Pakaluk argues, "the coronavirus lockdowns can teach almost as much about the Mass as the Council of Trent."

Back in February, I could not foresee that pious Catholics would be reduced to watching livestreamed Masses and attending parking-lot Communion services (if they were available). But I could say, even before this unexpected crisis, that the troubles facing the Catholic Church today can all be traced to a lack of reverence, a lack of commitment, a lack of the sense of wonder and awe that an earlier generation (before the advent of a misguided drive to put things in emasculated secular terms) called "fear of the Lord."

Hundreds of thousands of cradle Catholics have walked out the doors of the church over the past fifty years, planning never to return. We have watched them go. Untold thousands of potential converts have remained unmoved by what they see and have not entered. Our complacency in the face of this pastoral disaster is a scandal as destructive as the other scandals that have befallen our Church. Indeed, I contend that our lukewarmness has *caused* the other scandals. As I wrote in February:

> Something is terribly, terribly wrong—and has been wrong for years, because the mass exodus (no pun intended) began several decades ago. It should come as no surprise that, in an institution that lost its zeal for evangelization—its enthusiasm for its central mission—other signs of corruption would eventually appear.

Now it is no longer possible for Catholics to take the Mass and the Eucharist for granted. It is no longer rational to lapse into the presumption that the sacraments will always be there when we need them. Now is a propitious time to reflect on what it means to attend the re-presentation of Christ's sacrifice, to receive his Body and Blood, to be forgiven our sins.

The pastoral costs of the lockdown will, I fear, be enormous. Even a superficial survey of reactions reveals a sense of abandonment and demoralization. Many of the faithful have expressed their sense of loss in terms that resemble the mourning for a death or the trauma of abuse.

But our Lord can bring good out of any evil. This *could* be the time when chastened Catholics recover the sense of the sacred. Even if more parishes close and thousands more Catholics leave the Church, this *could* be the time when a great revival is triggered by a faithful few.

It doesn't take much to start a chain reaction. It only takes a critical mass.

10

Facing Our Challenges

Imagine that you had an opportunity to meet privately with someone you had always deeply admired: a world-class artist or politician or athlete or writer or entertainer whose work thrilled you. But when the day arrived for the meeting, the roads were icy. Would you still make the effort to go?

Or suppose you had the chance to take an active part in a major historic event, but an anonymous bomb threat was reported at the site of the event. Would you take the risk?

At the holy sacrifice of the Mass, Catholics have the opportunity for a private, intimate encounter with the Incarnate God, a chance to take an active part in the most important event in all history. In 2020 Catholics learned that attending Mass and receiving the Eucharist entailed a chance of contracting the Covid virus. The odds of infection were remote, and if an infection did occur, the chances that it would cause serious illness were more remote still.

How would the martyrs of the early Church have responded: those brave Christians who accepted death as the price for receiving the Eucharist? How about the Christians living under persecution, who risked their lives every time they attended

Mass? Not the way the pampered American Catholics of 2020 reacted, certainly.

If the Eucharist is the source and summit of our spiritual lives, attending Mass is surely worth a risk. To say otherwise is to suggest that our spiritual lives — our eternal souls — are less important than our short-term physical health. Regrettably, in 2020 many Catholics offered their neighbors a counter-witness: a suggestion that the prospect of eternal salvation is less important than a secure and healthy life on earth.

The Limits of Politics

In 1987, Lutheran cleric (soon to become a Catholic priest) Rev. Richard John Neuhaus wrote an important book entitled *The Catholic Moment.* Inspired by the public witness of Pope John Paul II, he argued that the time was ripe for the Catholic Church, especially in America, to make a crucial, transformative contribution to our public life. The Church, he remarked, is ideally suited for the task, with a history of sophisticated thought on the respective roles of Church and state, an understanding of the limits of secular authority that stretches back to St. Augustine's masterpiece, *The City of God.*

Today, Rev. Neuhaus wrote, our society faces a political crisis. "The crisis of this time and every time is the crisis of unbelief." And in answer to this crisis, he continued:

> Against the propensities of all states, and against the ideology of some states and movements, the Church must contend to secure social space for the personal and communal "aspiration to the infinite."

Ironically, a society whose citizens retain that "aspiration to the infinite" and realize that their government cannot solve all their problems is a society that can govern itself successfully. But when that aspiration is lost, that realization fades, and self-government becomes erratic, ineffectual, ultimately unsustainable.

Notice how, when the Covid crisis struck, Americans relied on governors and mayors and bureaucratic appointees, not on their elected representatives in legislatures, to set emergency guidelines. Notice how quickly legislators settled into debates on how much money the government should send to its citizens to offset the damage caused by the panic, rather than addressing the panic itself. Above all, notice how American public discourse in 2020 reached new lows of incivility, with political candidates routinely smearing each other rather than addressing their rivals' arguments.

Have we Americans lost the capacity for debating serious questions seriously, for resolving arguments of principle without violence? To restore and safeguard that capacity we need the witness of religious believers who understand the proper limits of any government's scope. Without that witness, without that understanding, it is no exaggeration to say that the American experiment with a republican form of government is doomed. "Our Constitution was made only for a moral and religious people," wrote John Adams. "It is wholly inadequate to the government of any other."

The Role of the Laity

For lay Catholics, the first and most important step toward recovery of the sacred is Sabbath observance: the preservation of one day each week that is given over to worship and leisure, deliberately set apart from the routine bustle of worldly affairs. Under any ordinary circumstances, for Catholics the Sabbath observance requires attendance at Sunday Mass. During the

Covid epidemic, bishops dispensed the lay faithful from that obligation. But they did not, and could not, dispense the faithful from the Sabbath observance.

The obligation to attend Mass on Sunday is a precept of the Church, which can be changed by a decision of the Church's leaders in the hierarchy. (In fact, it has been changed, obviously, for better or for worse: first by the decision to allow for an "anticipatory" Mass on Saturday that fulfills the Sunday obligation, then more recently by the general dispensations of 2020.) The order to "keep holy the Lord's Day," on the other hand, is a commandment of the almighty God, brought down by Moses from Mount Sinai, unchanged and unchangeable since that time.

To honor that commandment requires a special effort to make Sunday a day of rest, a day of prayer and contemplation. If the "anticipatory Mass" becomes an excuse for Catholics to check off their obligation and leave Sunday wide open for youth sports and shopping sprees and trips to the beach, that is an offense against God's commandment. If our friends and neighbors never notice that we treat Sundays differently, we have failed a key test as disciples.

And when we do attend Mass, do we — does our parish community — convey the message that this is the most important event of the week? "Good enough" liturgy is not good enough. If visitors are not impressed by the reverence of the liturgy, we have failed once again. Every serious Catholic should demand a reverent celebration of the Mass, with careful attention to the liturgical guidelines set by the universal Church. If they cannot find reverent and lawful liturgy in their home parishes, lay Catholics can and should look for it elsewhere.

Here I am assuming that at least in the United States, a practicing Catholic will ordinarily be able to find a church where the

Mass is celebrated on Sunday and the faithful are welcome to attend. That assumption — which no reasonable observer would have questioned before 2020 — was shattered when our bishops closed down the public celebration of the eucharistic liturgy. Still, if the same awful situation arose again, I would repeat the same advice: if they cannot find reverent and lawful liturgy in their home parishes or their home dioceses, lay Catholics can and should look for it elsewhere.

Should the faithful ignore a bishop's orders, then, if they are instructed not to attend Sunday Mass? Would it be sinfully disobedient to seek out an "underground" celebration of the Eucharistic liturgy — by a rogue priest, in an unauthorized chapel? Before answering that question, I would ask two questions of my own. First, did the bishop order the faithful *under obedience* to stay away from Mass? Second, does a bishop have the proper authority to issue such an order? Although I do not pretend to any expertise in canon law, I question whether a bishop's authority to regulate the liturgy allows him to *stop* the liturgy. Perhaps for that reason — because bishops were aware of the outer limits of their own authority to issue binding orders — I am not aware of any case in which an American bishop ordered the faithful not to attend Mass. But if a bishop did issue such an order, I for one would not hesitate to defy it. I would much rather be called to account, at the Last Judgment, for a lack of respect for my bishop, rather than for a violation of God's commandment.

A much less serious question — but one that troubled many lay Catholics in 2020 — is whether the faithful were obligated to obey a bishop's directive to wear masks in church. The question is less serious, certainly, because the Ten Commandments do not include a prohibition against masks. But again, the same questions arise: whether the bishop has made an order under obedience and whether a bishop has the authority to do so. The bishop unquestionably has the rightful authority to regulate the liturgy, and thus, for instance, to tell the priest-celebrant what vestments he should wear. But I am unaware of any serious argument that the bishop has the right to tell lay Catholics what they should wear when attending Mass — aside from the obvious stipulation (routinely ignored) that their dress should be appropriate to the solemnity of the ceremony.

The bishop also has the authority to teach on questions of morals and, in that capacity, he could instruct lay Catholics that they should not attend a community Mass if they are carrying a deadly infectious disease. But does any pastor have the right to tell an apparently healthy layman that he should absent himself from the sacraments because he *might* conceivably be infected, although he has no symptoms? (Can you, dear reader, *prove* that you are not, right now, infected with the bubonic plague?) The pastor's authority is not that of a physician, nor of a public health expert. If he issues rules based on the recommendations of civil officials, then those rules cannot command greater moral authority than that which the civic officials themselves enjoy.

The Duty of Clerics

Catholic priests are, first and foremost, ministers of the sacraments. They are also administrators and counselors and community leaders, but these latter are only incidental, secondary roles; in a crisis they can be dispensed with. We lay Catholics can operate our own parish plants if necessary; we can offer each other emotional and spiritual support; and we can certainly settle our community's public affairs without clerical involvement. But we cannot confect the Eucharist and we do not have the awesome power to absolve sins. For these absolute necessities of our spiritual lives, we need priests—and we need priests who understand *why* we need them.

We did not need priests to tell us how to avoid the Covid virus. Heaven knows we had enough "expert" advice on that score, coming to us from every direction. When we arrived in church on Sunday, we needed something different. We needed a respite from the world's obsession with this disease. We needed help to recover our "aspiration to the infinite."

Since a priest is the guardian of the sacraments, he contributes most to the health of the parish community when he worries more about the possibility of sacrilege than the possibility of infection—more about the danger of unworthy reception of the Eucharist than the danger of unsterile pews. Yes, a pastor should do his best to make the church a safe place. But he should often remind his people that Christians should not fear death, as long as they are living in a state of grace. He should certainly tell parishioners who are sick to stay home until they are healthy again. But he might also counsel hypochondriacs to examine their consciences and advise healthy young people not to use an unrealistic fear of disease as an excuse for ignoring spiritual duties.

The Covid crisis has exposed a serious division within the Catholic Church. I should say rather that the year 2020 shone a high-intensity spotlight on a problem within Catholicism that serious commentators have been discussing for decades. When some Catholics see the reception of the sacraments as the most important work of the Church and others see the administration of the sacraments as an unacceptable danger to the faithful, we have reached an impasse. We can no longer paper over the division; we cannot pretend that the differences are superficial. Regrettably, most Church leaders remain committed to that pretense—unwilling or unable to recognize that an era of crisis calls for a bold and clear response.

Realistically speaking, we lay Catholics cannot hope to achieve a revival of Catholic spirituality without the support of our bishops. So we must plead with them, coax them, cajole them, press them, even shame them if it is necessary, until we have convinced them to take on the bold leadership we need to restore our Church.

Quiet Confidence

We have endured a terribly difficult year. Our society is torn apart by fear: fear of disease, fear of others, fear for the future. We all face the challenge of maintaining our inner peace, our confidence, our hope. To do so, Christians must bear constantly in mind—and convey to others as well—the enduring truth that Jesus is Lord.

Epidemics may come, and wars may rage, and governments may teeter and fall, but if our sights are set on the Lord, we can maintain the proper perspective. If we can—if we could only!—persuade our neighbors to set their sights on Jesus, too, then our society can still be saved from what seems now to be a death spiral into fear and hatred and despair.

We profess that Jesus is Lord. We want our neighbors to accept that truth. We know that they will be better off—infinitely, eternally better off—for accepting it. But since we cannot convert the world by our own efforts, we need to keep two things in mind:

First, *Jesus* is in control. We are not. We can pray and work for the coming of the Kingdom, but we cannot schedule its arrival.

Second, Jesus *is* in control. It matters—it matters very much—whether we believe that, whether our neighbors and friends believe that, whether our society is built upon that belief. But whether or not we believe it, or our neighbors believe it, or our society acknowledges it, it remains a fact. Jesus *is* in control, and therein lies our hope.

Fear All around Us

Every morning, for the better part of a year now, a headline in the local newspaper has called attention to the "record" number of Covid casualties.

The headlines are evidently written so as to maximize the readers' alarm. If the death rate decreases, the headline points to the number of hospitalizations. If hospitalizations drop, the headline points to the number of positive tests. If that figure sags, the headline notes the cumulative total of deaths—which of course can only increase.

Granted, the Covid epidemic is a very big story. But every sentient reader already knows about the crisis; an occasional reminder about the statistics would surely serve. These daily headlines are clearly unnecessary. So why do they continue? Because fear is powerful; fear sells.

The newspaper is not the only source of fear, of course. Every day the ordinary American encounters reminders of the Covid menace: on radio and television broadcasts, on highway signs, in customer-service announcements piped into supermarkets, and of course on the social media. Invitations to fear surround us.

We stay home from church out of fear. Not just any fear, but specifically, fear of Covid. We are not afraid of being killed by a meteor, or a drive-by shooting, or a wild animal, or an automobile accident on the way to church. Any one of those tragic outcomes is a possibility, and a fatal accident is more likely than a Covid death. But we have learned to dismiss or at least to tolerate these other risks, whereas we have been trained to be terrified by the threat of Covid.

So if we do conquer our fears and go to Sunday Mass, we are easily distracted by the sneezes of someone in the next pew. Or, if we eschew masks, we are distracted by the concern that someone will come reprimand us for not following the emergency guidelines. So we have a new source of distraction at prayer — as if we didn't already have distractions enough.

Fear as a Distraction

St. Teresa of Avila referred to the deep well of distractions as "the madwoman running around the house," constantly proposing new thoughts to interfere with prayer. The mind rummages around its dusty recesses and finds new worries, new grudges, new daydreams: anything to distract the faithful from a simple conversation with the Lord. Fear is a powerful motivation and a powerful distraction.

In this case — the Covid epidemic — fear is especially damaging to the spiritual life because it not only distracts us from prayer but tempts us to look upon our neighbors as threats to our health. Thus, we can be discouraged from charitable works and, particularly, from those charitable works that would bring us into direct contact with the people in need — which is to say, the most beneficial and Christ-like forms of charity.

And as if that weren't enough, the results of our fear — the universal lockdown of society — has given us excuses to stop doing our own work, to neglect our vocational and professional responsibilities. It's so easy to procrastinate when the office is closed! It's so tempting to let projects wait until we return to normalcy. There are so many reasons — good reasons, many of them—why work will run more smoothly when the lockdown is over. So we wait, and our work goes undone.

Rather than doing our work, we spend our time complaining about the obstacles that (we claim) make the work more difficult. Or we spend that time arguing online about the severity of the epidemic, or the need for a lockdown, or the experts' predictions—rather than doing what we could do, ourselves, to use our time productively.

The Proven Antidote

Think of all these unproductive responses as distractions or temptations, and you realize how skillfully Satan has used this epidemic to damage our spiritual lives, using the poisonous weapon of fear. The antidote, for a Christian, is both obvious and near at hand: a confident reliance on God, an abandonment to His holy will.

Is Covid a dangerous disease? Absolutely! But once we have taken reasonable precautions, it is essential for us as Christians to stop worrying about a force that we cannot control. In Shakespeare's *Julius Caesar*, when Calpurnia warns Caesar about his fate, he replies:

> Cowards die many times before their deaths;
> The valiant never taste of death but once.
> Of all the wonders that I yet have heard,
> It seems to me most strange that men should fear;
> Seeing that death, a necessary end,
> Will come when it will come.

Caesar did not dismiss his wife's troubled dreams but, ultimately, he rejected her advice to stay home, "in shame of cowardice." And yes, Caesar did die—but only once. He did not waste his time, distracted by useless fears.

Contagious Faith

If Shakespeare's pagan dictator could face his fate stoically, how much more reason do we Christians have to set aside our fears, knowing that we are in the hands of a loving and all-powerful Father? Caesar, a rational man, expected to die. Whereas we, having an understanding that goes beyond reason—inspired by the supernatural gift of hope—can confidently expect to live forever.

About the Author

Philip F. Lawler is the founder (in 1995) and editor of Catholic World News, the first English-language Catholic news service operating on the Internet. He is also the program director of the Center for the Restoration of Christian Culture at Thomas More College in New Hampshire.

Born and raised in the Boston area, he attended Harvard College, graduating with honors in government in 1972. He did graduate work in political philosophy at the University of Chicago before entering a career in journalism.

Mr. Lawler has served as director of studies for the Heritage Foundation, a conservative think tank based in Washington, DC; as founder and president of a national organization of Catholic laity; and as editor of *Crisis Magazine*. In 1986, he became the first layman to edit *The Pilot*, the Boston archdiocesan newspaper. From 1993 through 2005, he was editor of the international monthly magazine *Catholic World Report*.

Mr. Lawler has been active in political campaigns, as a speechwriter and organizer, on the local, state, and national levels. He was an honorary member of the inauguration committees for President Ronald Reagan in 1984 and for President George

Bush in 1988. In 2000, he himself was a candidate for the U.S. Senate, running against Senator Edward Kennedy.

Mr. Lawler is the author or editor of ten books on political and religious topics, including *The Faithful Departed*, on the decline of Catholic influence in Boston; *Lost Shepherd*, a candid appraisal of Pope Francis; and most recently, *Smoke of Satan: How Corrupt and Cowardly Bishops Betrayed Christ, His Church, and the Faithful . . . and What Can Be Done about It*. His essays, book reviews, and editorial columns have appeared in more than one hundred newspapers around the United States and abroad, including the *Wall Street Journal*, the *Los Angeles Times*, the *Washington Post*, and the *Boston Globe*.

He and his wife, Leila (the author of *God Has No Grandchildren* and the forthcoming *Summa Domestica*), have seven children and (at last count) sixteen grandchildren. The Lawlers live in central Massachusetts.

CRISIS Publications

Sophia Institute Press awards the privileged title "CRISIS Publications" to a select few of our books that address contemporary issues at the intersection of politics, culture, and the Church with clarity, cogency, and force and that are also destined to become all-time classics.

CRISIS Publications are *direct*, explaining their principles briefly, simply, and clearly to Catholics in the pews, on whom the future of the Church depends. The time for ambiguity or confusion is long past.

CRISIS Publications are *contemporary*, born of our own time and circumstances and intended to become significant statements in current debates, statements that serious Catholics cannot ignore, regardless of their prior views.

CRISIS Publications are *classical*, addressing themes and enunciating principles that are valid for all ages and cultures. Readers will turn to them time and again for guidance in other days and different circumstances.

CRISIS Publications are *spirited*, entering contemporary debates with gusto to clarify issues and demonstrate how those issues can be resolved in a way that enlivens souls and the Church.

We welcome engagement with our readers on current and future CRISIS Publications. Please pray that this imprint may help to resolve the crises embroiling our Church and society today.